Transition to Attic Greek

A Supplement to
A Reading Course in Homeric Greek

Transition to Attic Greek

A Supplement to
A Reading Course in Homeric Greek

by

Raymond V. Schoder, S.J., M.A., Ph.D.
Vincent C. Horrigan, S.J., M.A.

Revised, with additional materials by
Leslie Collins Edwards

focus An Imprint of
Hackett Publishing Company
Indianapolis/Cambridge

From *Transition to Attic Greek* by Raymond V. Schoder and Vincent C. Horrigan. © 1949 by Chicago Province, Society of Jesus. Permission to reprint granted by the publisher.

This book has been reproduced with permission of the copyright holder and the proper royalty fees have been paid. Any reproduction of this material is illegal under copyright law.

Additional materials copyright © 2006 Focus Publishing/R. Pullins Co. Inc.

Cover: "Book 13" The Iliad Series 40" x 30" (mixed media on paper) © 2003 Merle Mainelli Poulton. *For My Parents.*

Previously published by Focus Publishing / R. Pullins Company
Focus An Imprint of
Hackett Publishing Company
www.hackettpublishing.com
P.O. Box 44937
Indianapolis, Indiana 46244-0937
Printed in the United States of America

All rights reserved

ISBN-13: 978-1-58510-196-2

18 17 16 15   2 3 4 5 6

Table Of Contents

Foreword 1
How to Use This Book 3
Part I: General Principles 5
Part II: Declension 7
Part III: Conjugation 15
Part IV: Syntax 25
Part V: Vocabulary 35
Answers to Exercises 37

Foreword

It is important to understand the purpose of this book.

It is not a complete Grammar of Attic Greek and is not intended to displace the standard Attic Grammars, which the student will have to consult frequently in his further reading. Nor is it a general transition from Homeric to Attic Greek suitable for anyone who has begun the study of Greek with Homer. Of course, it will be of some help, both as a Grammar and as a general transition, to anyone who wishes to use it as such; but its real purpose is more specific.

This book has been written for that particular group of students who have completed the authors' *Reading Course in Homeric Greek* and now wish to take a course in which an Attic author is read. Most editions available presume an Attic background. Although the more logical approach to Greek literature is through the study of Homer and although the student of Homeric Greek will have the advantage of a linguistic and cultural background not shared by those who begin at once with Attic, nevertheless he will naturally be at some disadvantage in the beginning in handling purely Attic forms. Often enough explanations will be offered of points which are obvious to the Homeric student while other things which are unfamiliar to him are taken for granted. *Transition to Attic Greek* is intended to be a handy reference book to assist the student in tracking down these unfamiliar peculiarities of Attic.

A thorough investigation was made of the most popular beginners' books based on the Attic dialect. Any forms or points of grammar taught in these books but not contained in the Homer course were noted down, systematized, and are presented thoroughly but as simply as possible in the transition book. It is possible, therefore, with the aid of this book, for the student of Homeric Greek to add to his general knowledge of Greek whatever in the way of forms and syntax he may have missed by not beginning Greek with the Attic dialect. Thus he can continue his reading of Greek literature with the confidence and the comfort that the difficulties he will inevitably encounter must be met likewise by all his peers.

R.V.S. and V.C.H., 1949

Cover Design

Execias' fifth-century vase painting of Dionysus, the wine-god, crossing over from Asia Minor to the Greek mainland and bringing with him a new culture, appropriately symbolizes the transition from Homeric to Attic Greek that is the aim of this book.

(From a kylix vase, now in Munich)

How to Use This Book

His first sight of the transition book may leave the student with a feeling akin to panic. It does indeed look rather formidable. And it would be formidable if it were necessary to sit down and learn all of it at one time. Fortunately, such is not the case.

In the first place, this is primarily a reference book, written not so much for class use as for private consultation in the course of reading. Many things are best learned when met in context, and mastery of them may be postponed legitimately until looking them up several times has added them to one's permanent equipment. The forms of the irregular verbs, for example, cause almost everybody trouble for a considerable period of time before they are finally and certainly assimilated.

Since this is a reference book, the charts are more complete than might be necessary for immediate teaching. Even when the various Attic forms can be reduced to a fairly simple rule the whole line-up of forms is given anyway in order to settle any doubts in applying the rule and to facilitate the discovery of a form that is causing difficulty. A whole page is devoted to listing the possible contractions of verb stems in α, ε, or ο, although these contractions can and should be deduced from the general rules for contraction.

Secondly, much of the matter in this book is already familiar, being either the same as in Homer or so similar that one would hardly notice the difference in reading. All that is necessary is to note carefully the place or places where Attic differs from what is already known. For example, most of the endings of the regular verb listed here are the same as in Homer; only the few new ones need be studied. In order to make it easier to spot the exclusively Attic or new forms, they have been put in bold type. On the other hand, Homeric forms which are not found in Attic are put in square brackets. In other places both the Homeric and the Attic forms are given in parallel columns to give a quick picture of just which changes occur.

We do not mean to discourage the ambitious student from mastering at once all that is contained in the book, especially if it is taken in class and he has the advantage of direction by the teacher. On the contrary, the more the student can learn beforehand the easier and more pleasant will be all his further reading. It is for those who cannot spend a great deal of time on the transition book that we offer the following suggestions.

If you have time for nothing else, at least familiarize yourself thoroughly with the arrangement of the book so that you know just what it contains and where to put your finger on any forms or rules you may wish to look up. Notice that the matter is divided into five main divisions: general principles, declensions, conjugations, syntax (that of the verb arranged both according to construction and according to mood), and vocabulary (listing the particular memory words from the Homer course which change in passing over into Attic). Reading through the book several times fairly carefully, noticing just what each chart deals with, will enable you to use it profitably and with the least loss of time.

The next step would be to learn as thoroughly as time permits the rules that summarize the important points of each section. If these are intelligently grasped, it will not be necessary to pay much attention to the detailed charts which illustrate their application. Of particular importance in this regard are the rules for vowel-contraction in Attic found under General Principles. Any amount of time spent on them will be amply repaid.

The declensions and the conjugation of the regular verb are close to the Homeric forms you already know, and are, of course, of considerable importance. After them you might go over the syntax of the Attic definite article; although some of the rules are not of great moment, the high frequency of the article makes a general knowledge of its uses imperative.

The syntax of the verb arranged according to constructions is probably the better for purposes of initial study; the other is more convenient for reference. As regards the vocabulary lists, not much time need be spent on them. A merely passive knowledge, that is, the ability to recognize the word when it occurs in context, will be sufficient for the first stages in Attic reading. These and other such items can be taken more or less thoroughly as circumstances permit.

For a fuller treatment of the matter presented in this transition book and for the many less important details that are not included in it, you will find the following Grammars useful:

Smyth, Herbert Weir and Gordon M. Messing. *Greek Grammar*. (Harvard University Press. Revised Edition 2004) The most complete; at the same time very clear and with excellent indexes for reference.
Goodwin, William W. *A Greek Grammar*. (Wipf and Stock Publishers 2003)
Morwood, James. *The Oxford Grammar of Classical Greek*. (Oxford University Press 2003)
Goodwin, William W. *Syntax of the Moods and Tenses of the Greek Verb*. (Wipf and Stock Publishers 2003)
Denniston, J. D. *The Greek Particles*. (Hackett Publishing. 2nd Edition 1996)
Marinone, N. *All the Greek Verbs* (=*Tutti i Verbi Greci*). (Duckworth Publishing 1985)

Part I
GENERAL PRINCIPLES

1. DIALECTS. Ancient literary Greek was written in three main dialects: Aeolic, Doric, and Ionic. By far the most important was Ionic, which was itself subdivided into four divisions: Epic, New Ionic, Attic, and Koine. Here is a list (for reference) of the principal authors arranged according to their dialect. It must be noted, however, that the dialects were by no means mutually exclusive; Attic poetry, for example, has many Epic and a fair number of Doric forms.

- A. Aeolic
    1. Alcaeus (7th to 6th century BC) Lyric Poet
    2. Sappho (7th to 6th century BC) Lyric Poet
    3. Anacreon (6th century BC) Lyric Poet
- B. Doric
    1. Stesichorus (6th century BC) Lyric Poet
    2. Pindar (6th to 5th century BC) Lyric Poet
    3. Bacchylides (5th century BC) Lyric Poet
    4. Simonides (6th to 5th century BC) Lyric Poet
    5. Theocritus (3rd century BC) Bucolic Poet
- C. Ionic
    1. Epic:
        a. Homer (8th century BC) Epic Poet
        b. Hesiod (8th to 7th century BC) Didactic Poet
    2. New Ionic:
        a. Archilochus (7th century BC) Lyric Poet
        b. Herodotus (5th century BC) Historian
        c. Hippocrates (5th century BC) Medical Writer
    3. Attic:
        a. Aeschylus (525 - 456 BC) Tragic Poet
        b. Sophocles (496 - 406 BC) Tragic Poet
        c. Euripides (480 - 406 BC) Tragic Poet
        d. Aristophanes (c.450-386 BC) Comic Poet
        e. Thucydides (c.460 - 400 BC) Historian
        f. Xenophon (c.430 - 355 BC) Historian
        g. Lysias (c.458 - 380 BC) Orator
        h. Isocrates (436 - 338 BC) Orator
        i. Aeschines (c.397-322 BC) Orator
        j. Demosthenes (384 - 322 BC) Orator
        k. Plato (429 - 347 BC) Philosopher
    4. Koine:
        a. Septuagint (c.250 BC) Translation of Old Testament
        b. New Testament (c.42 - 96 AD)
        c. Polybius (c.200 - 118 BC) Historian
        d. Diodorus (1st century BC) Historian
        e. Strabo (c.64 BC - 19 AD) Geographer
        f. Dionysius of Halicarnassus (c.60 BC - 5 AD) Rhetorician and Historian
        g. Josephus (c.37 - 100 AD) Jewish Historian

h. Plutarch (c.46 - 121 AD) Historian and Essayist
i. Arrian (c.86 - 160 AD) Historian
j. Lucian (c.120 - 180 AD) Rhetorician and Literary Critic
k. Cassius Dio (c.164 - 230 AD) Historian

N.B. Dionysius and Lucian, though writing in the Koine period, imitated Attic usage in their style and language.

2. STRESS. In reading Homer you have been accustomed to stress syllables according to their quantity and their position in the metrical pattern. The same practice prevails in the reading of Attic poetry. In Attic prose, however, there is a wide-spread custom of stressing words according to the position of the pitch mark (although the Attic authors themselves did not do so). Thus in Homeric Greek you learned to stress ἄνθρωπος on the penult, ἄν-θρω-πος. When reading Attic prose you may if you wish stress the word where the pitch mark is, no matter on what syllable it stands, e.g., ἄν-θρω-πος.

3. AUGMENT. In Attic prose the rule is that past tenses of the indicative <u>must always be augmented</u>. For this reason the 3rd principal part of the verb is usually listed in its augmented form, for example: γιγνώσκω, γνώσομαι, ἔγνων; λύω, λύσω, ἔλυσα. Remember that this augment must be cut off in the aorist subjunctive, optative, imperative, infinitive, and participle.

4. CONTRACTION. A very important characteristic of the Attic dialect is its tendency to contract contiguous vowels. Hence it is necessary to study the question now more fully than was done in the Homer course. The rules you have already learned hold good also in Attic except that ε + ο, which contracts to ευ in Homer, becomes ου in Attic. The chart of the possible combinations will be helpful in testing your grasp of the rules.

<u>Rules for Contraction:</u>
(1) α+α-sound is absorbed.
     α+ε-sound =ᾱ (subscribe ι)
     α+ο-sound =ω (subscribe ι)

(2) ε+α =η   <u>Exception</u>: ε+α =α in 1st. decl. acc. pl. and 2nd decl. n. pl.
     ε+ε =ει
     ε+ο =ου
     ε+η, ω, or any diphthong is absorbed.

(3) ο+α, η, ω =ω
     ο+ε, ο, ου =ου
     ο+ι-diphthong =οι   <u>Exception</u>: ο+ῳ =ῳ

TABLE OF CONTRACTIONS

+	α	ᾳ	αι	ε	ει	η	ῃ	ο	οι	ου	ω	ῳ
α	= ᾱ	= ᾳ	= αι	= ᾱ	= ᾳ	= ᾱ	= ᾳ	= ω	= ῳ	= ω	= ω	*
ε	= η (ᾱ)	*	= αι	= ει	= ει	= η	= ῃ	= ου	= οι	= ου	= ω	= ῳ
ο	= ω	*	= αι	= ου	= οι	= ω	= ῳ	= ου	= οι	= ου	= ω	= ῳ

* These contractions are not found.

N.B. 1. Whenever in the 3rd. decl. both the nom. pl. and the acc. pl. contract, the acc. is <u>always</u> the same as the nom., regardless of rule. (See examples on page 10.)

2. In the 2nd. sg. mid. of verbs, -ε(σ)αι is usually found as -η in the text of the tragic poets, as -ει in prose and comedy.

Part II
DECLENSION

Note: The vocative case is omitted in this treatment. It follows the rules already learned.

1st Declension

1. All nouns, adjs., and ptcs. take -ων and -αις in the gen. and dat. plural.
2. Nouns ending in α (or ας) preceded by ε, ι, or ρ keep the α throughout the sg.
3. Adjs. and ptcs. have α in the nom. sg. after ε, ι, or ρ (even in contraction!) and keep it throughout the sg.; otherwise they have η.
4. Masculine nouns take -ου in the gen. sg.
5. Some nouns and adjs., and all ptcs., with stems in ε-, α-, or ο- undergo contraction.

	δίκη *justice*		ἡδεῖα *sweet*		ναύτης *sailor*		χρύσεα *golden*		ὁράουσα *seeing*	
	Homeric	Attic	Homeric	Attic	Homeric	Attic	Homeric	Attic	Homeric	Attic
	δικ-	δικ-	ἡδει-	ἡδει-	ναυτ-	ναυτ-	χρυσε-	χρυσ-	ὁρα-	ὁρ-
Sg. N	η	η	α	α	ης	ης	η	η	ουσα	ῶσα
G	ης	ης	[ης]	**ας**	[ᾱο, εω]	**ου**	ης	ης	ούσης	ώσης
D	ῃ	ῃ	[ῃ]	**ᾳ**	ῃ	ῃ	ῃ	ῃ	ούσῃ	ώσῃ
A	ην	ην	αν	αν	ην	ην	ην	ην	ουσαν	ῶσαν
Pl. N	αι	αι	αι	αι	αι	αι	αι	αι	ουσαι	ῶσαι
G	[ᾱων]	**ων**	[ᾱων]	**ων**	[ᾱων]	**ων**	[ᾱων]	**ων**	ουσᾶων	ωσῶν
D	[ῃσ(ι)]	**αις**	[ῃσ(ι)]	**αις**	[ῃσ(ι)]	**αις**	[ῃσ(ι)]	**αις**	ούσῃσι	ώσαις
A	ᾱς	ᾱς	ᾱς	ᾱς	ᾱς	ᾱς	ᾱς	ᾱς	ούσᾱς	ώσᾱς

2nd Declension

1. -οιο is not used in the gen. sg., nor is -οισι used in the dat. pl.
2. Some nouns and adjs. undergo contraction.
3. All ptcs. with stems in α-, ε-, or ο- contract.

	θεός *god*		χρύσεος *golden*		ὁραόμενος *being seen*	
	Homeric	Attic	Homeric	Attic	Homeric	Attic
	θε-	θε-	χρυσε-	χρυσ-	ὁρα-	ὁρ-
Sg. N	ος	ος	ος	ους	ομενος	ωμενος
G	ου [οιο]	ου	ου [οιο]	ου	ομενου	ωμενου
D	ῳ	ῳ	ῳ	ῳ	ομενῳ	ωμενῳ
A	ον	ον	ον	ουν	ομενον	ωμενον
Pl. N	οι	οι	οι	οι	ομενοι	ωμενοι
G	ων	ων	ων	ων	ομενων	ωμενοι
D	οις [οισι]	οις	οις [οισι]	οις	ομενοις	ωμενους
A	ους	ους	ους	ους	ομενους	ωμενους

3rd Declension

1. Endings are the same, except:
   (1) shortened form of dat. pl. is always used.
   (2) -ς is used for -ας in acc. pl. of stems ending in υ-.

2. Nouns with stems in ι- and some with stems in υ- :
   (1) change stem-vowel to ε-, except in the acc. sg.
   (2) lengthen gen. sg. ending.

3. Nouns with stems in ευ- :
   (1) change stem-vowel to ε-, except in the dat. pl.
   (2) lengthen gen. sg. ending.

4. Contraction: which 3rd-declension forms contract and which do not is a complicated problem. These rules will help you to remember:
   I. Nouns
      (1) ε- and α- stems contract whenever possible.
      (2) ι- and υ- stems which change to ε- contract nom./acc. pl. only.
      (3) ευ- stems contract nom. pl. only.
   II. Adjectives
      (1) in -ης, -ες contract whenever possible.
      (2) in -υς, -εια, -υ contract masculine nom./acc. pl. only.
      (3) comparatives in -ων, -ον *sometimes* contract m. acc. sg. and nom./acc. plural.
   III. Participles
      (1) All participles contract whenever possible.

Third declension paradigms (forms showing variation from Homeric in bold):

ἄναξ *king*

	Homeric	Attic
Sg.N	ἄναξ	ἄναξ
G	ἄνακτ-ος	ἄνακτ-ος
D	ἄνακτ-ι	ἄνακτ-ι
A	ἄνακτ-α	ἄνακτ-α
Pl.N	ἄνακτ-ες	ἄνακτ-ες
G	ἀνάκτ-ων	ἀνάκτ-ων
D	ἀνάκτ-εσσι, ἄναξι	ἄναξι
A	ἄνακτ-ας	ἄνακτ-ας

ἰχθύς *fish*

	Homeric	Attic
Sg.N	ἰχθύς	ἰχθύς
G	ἰχθύ-ος	ἰχθύ-ος
D	ἰχθυ-ῖ	**ἰχθύ-ϊ**
A	ἰχθύ-ν	ἰχθύ-ν
Pl.N	ἰχθύ-ες	ἰχθύ-ες
G	ἰχθύ-ων	ἰχθύ-ων
D	ἰχθύ-σι	ἰχθύ-σι
A	ἰχθύ-ας	**ἰχθῦ-ς**

πόλις *city*

	Homeric	Attic
Sg.N	πόλις	πόλις
G	πόλι-ος	**πόλε-ως**
D	πόλι-ι	**πόλε-ι**
A	πόλι-ν	πόλι-ν
Pl.N	πόλι-ες	**πόλεις**
G	πολί-ων	**πόλε-ων**
D	πολί-εσσι, πόλι-σι	**πόλε-σι**
A	πόλι-ας	**πόλεις**

ἄστυ *town* (original stem = ἀστυ-)

	Homeric	Attic
Sg.N	ἄστυ	ἄστυ
G	ἄστε-ος	**ἄστε-ως**
D	ἄστε-ϊ	**ἄστε-ι**
A	ἄστυ	ἄστυ
Pl.N	ἄστε-α	**ἄστη**
G	ἀστέ-ων	**ἄστε-ων**
D	ἀστέ-εσι, ἄστε-σι	ἄστε-σι
A	ἄστε-α	**ἄστη**

βασιλεύς *king* (original stem = βασιλευ-)

	Homeric	Attic
Sg.N	βασιλεύς	βασιλεύς
G	βασιλῆ-ος	**βασιλέ-ως**
D	βασιλῆ-ι	**βασιλε-ῖ**
A	βασιλῆ-α	**βασιλέ-α**
Pl.N	βασιλῆ-ες	**βασιλεῖς**
G	βασιλή-ων	**βασιλέ-ων**
D	βασιλή-εσσι	**βασιλεῦ-σι**
A	βασιλῆ-ας	**βασιλέ-ας**

ἔπος *word*

	Homeric	Attic
Sg.N	ἔπος	ἔπος
G	ἔπε-ος	**ἔπους**
D	ἔπε-ϊ	**ἔπει**
A	ἔπος	ἔπος
Pl.N	ἔπε-α	**ἔπη**
G	ἐπέ-ων	**ἐπῶν**
D	ἐπέ-εσσι, ἔπε-σι	ἔπε-σι
A	ἔπε-α	**ἔπη**

γέρας *prize*

	Homeric	Attic
Sg.N	γέρας	γέρας
G	γέρα-ος	**γέρως**
D	γέρα-ϊ	**γέραι**
A	γέρας	γέρας
Pl.N	γέρα-α	**γέρᾱ**
G	γερά-ων	**γερῶν**
D	γέρα-σι	γέρα-σι
A	γέρα-α	**γέρᾱ**

ἀληθής, -ές *true*

	Homeric (m/f)	(n)	Attic (m/f)	(n)
Sg.N	ἀληθής	ἀληθές	ἀληθής	ἀληθές
G	ἀληθέ-ος	ἀληθέ-ος	**ἀληθοῦς**	**ἀληθοῦς**
D	ἀληθέ-ϊ	ἀληθέ-ϊ	**ἀληθεῖ**	**ἀληθεῖ**
A	ἀληθέ-α	ἀληθές	**ἀληθῆ**	ἀληθές
Pl.N	ἀληθέ-ες	ἀληθέ-α	**ἀληθεῖς**	**ἀληθῆ**
G	ἀληθέ-ων	ἀληθέ-ων	**ἀληθῶν**	**ἀληθῶν**
D	ἀληθέ-σι	ἀληθέ-σι	ἀληθέ-σι	ἀληθέ-σι
A	ἀληθέ-ας	ἀληθέ-α	**ἀληθεῖς**	**ἀληθῆ**

ἡδύς, -εῖα, -ύ *sweet* (see 1st decl. chart for fem.)

	Homeric		Attic	
	(m)	(n)	(m)	(n)
Sg.N	ἡδύς	ἡδύ	ἡδύς	ἡδύ
G	ἡδέ-ος	ἡδέ-ος	ἡδέ-ος	ἡδέ-ος
D	ἡδέ-ι	ἡδέ-ι	**ἡδε-ῖ**	**ἡδε-ῖ**
A	ἡδύ-ν	ἡδύ	ἡδύ-ν	ἡδύ
Pl.N	ἡδέ-ες	ἡδέ-α	**ἡδεῖς**	ἡδέ-α
G	ἡδέ-ων	ἡδέ-ων	ἡδέ-ων	ἡδέ-ων
D	ἡδέ-σι	ἡδέ-σι	ἡδέ-σι	ἡδέ-σι
A	ἡδέ-ας	ἡδέ-α	**ἡδεῖς**	ἡδέ-α

μείζων, -ον *greater*

	Homeric		Attic	
	(m)	(n)	(m)	(n)
Sg.N	μείζων	μεῖζον	μείζων	μεῖζον
G	μείζον-ος	μείζον-ος	μείζον-ος	μείζον-ος
D	μείζον-ι	μείζον-ι	μείζον-ι	μείζον-ι
A	μείζον-α	μεῖζον	**μείζω**	μεῖζον
Pl.N	μείζον-ες	μείζον-α	**μείζους**	**μείζω**
G	μειζόν-ων	μειζόν-ων	μειζόν-ων	μειζόν-ων
D	μείζο-σι	μείζο-σι	μείζο-σι	μείζο-σι
A	μείζον-ας	μείζον-α	**μείζους**	**μείζω**

ὁραων *seeing*

	Homeric	Attic
	(m)	(n)
Sg.N	ὁράων	**ὁρῶν**
G	ὁράοντος	**ὁρῶντος**
D	ὁράοντι	**ὁρῶντι**
A	ὁράοντα	**ὁρῶντα**
Pl.N	ὁράοντες	**ὁρῶντες**
G	ὁραόντων	**ὁρώντων**
D	ὁραόντεσσι, ὁράουσι	**ὁρῶσι**
A	ὁράοντας	**ὁρῶντας**

IRREGULAR NOUNS Homer uses various forms of these words. Only the following occur in Attic:

	ox/cow (m/f)	*ship* (f)	*father* (m)
Sg.N	βοῦς	**ναῦς**	πατήρ
G	βο-ός	**νε-ώς**	πατρ-ός
D	βο-ΐ	νη-ί	πατρ-ί
A	βοῦ-ν	**ναῦ-ν**	πατέρ-α
Pl.N	βό-ες	νῆ-ες	πατέρ-ες
G	βο-ῶν	νε-ῶν	πατέρ-ων
D	βου-σί	**ναυ-σί**	πατρά-σι
A	βοῦ-ς	**ναῦ-ς**	πατέρ-ας

Exercise on the Attic 1st and 2nd declensions. Give the forms named after the colon. (Answers on last page)

1. ἡδονή, *pleasure*: gen. pl.
2. νεανίας, *young man*: acc. sg.
3. νόος, *mind*: acc. sg. (contract)
4. πέτρα, *rock*: dat. sg.
5. χάλκεος, *bronze*: f.acc.pl. (contract)
6. ἀργύρεος, *silver*: n.acc.pl. (contract)
7. εἰρήνη, *peace*: dat. pl.
8. ποιέων, *making*: f. gen. pl.
9. ποιεόμενος, *being made*: n. gen. sg.
10. οὐτάων, *wounding*: f. dat. pl.

Exercise on the 3rd declension. Referring to the 3rd declension paradigms above, give the Attic forms of the following:

1. πλείων, -ον *more*: f. acc. pl.
2. δυσμενής, -ές *hostile*: n. acc. pl.
3. γῆρας, -αος *old age*: gen. pl.
4. φύσις, -ιος *nature*: gen. sg.
5. ὀξύς, -εῖα, -ύ *sharp*: n. gen. pl.
6. ποιέων *making*: m. dat. sg.
7. τοκεύς, -ῆος *parent*: nom. pl.
8. νηῦς, νηός *ship*: nom. pl.
9. ἄστυ, -εος *town*: gen. sg.
10. παῖς, παιδός *child*: acc. sg.
11. εὐρύς, -εῖα, -ύ *wide*: n. nom. pl.
12. ἄλγος, -εος *pain*: nom. pl.
13. ἀρείων, -ον *better*: n. acc. sg.
14. ἰχθύς, -ύος *fish*: acc. pl.
15. χθών, χθονός *earth*: acc. sg.
16. μῆκος, -εος *length*: gen. pl.
17. βοῦς, βοός *cow*: acc. pl.
18. οὐτάων *wounding*: n. dat. pl.
19. σῶμα, -ατος *body*: dat. pl.
20. βασιλεύς, -ῆος *king*: acc. pl.
21. μελιηδής, -ές *honey-sweet*: f. acc. sg.
22. διοτρεφής, -ές *Zeus-cherished*: f. gen. sg.
23. ὠκύς, -εῖα, -ύ *swift*: m. acc. pl.
24. ποιμήν, -ένος *shepherd*: acc. sg.
25. τοκεύς, -ῆος *parent*: gen. sg.
26. πατήρ, πατρός *father*: dat. pl.
27. γῆρας, -αος *old age*: acc. pl.
28. παχύς, -εῖα, -ύ *thick*: m. nom. pl.
29. ἄστυ, -εος *town*: acc. pl.
30. κράτος, -εος *strength*: gen. sg.

Irregular Pronouns

1. ὁ, ἡ, τό, a weak demonstrative in Homer, is used as the definite article in Attic Greek. The same changes in the forms occur as in the 1st and 2nd declensions. Notice also that ται and τοι are not used.

The Definitive Article: ὁ, ἡ, τό *the*

	Homeric			Attic		
	(m)	(f)	(n)	(m)	(f)	(n)
Sg. N	ὁ	ἡ	τό	ὁ	ἡ	τό
G	τοῦ [τοῖο]	τῆς	τοῦ [τοῖο]	τοῦ	τῆς	τοῦ
D	τῷ	τῇ	τῷ	τῷ	τῇ	τῷ
A	τόν	τήν	τό	τόν	τήν	τό
Pl. N	οἱ [τοι]	αἱ [ται]	τά	οἱ	αἱ	τά
G	τῶν	[τάων]	τῶν	τῶν	**τῶν**	τῶν
D	τοῖς [τοῖσι]	[τῇσ(ι)]	τοῖς [τοῖσι]	τοῖς	**ταῖς**	τοῖς
A	τούς	τάς	τά	τούς	τάς	τά

2. The personal pronouns in Attic use ου for ευ, and undergo contraction in a number of places. In Attic oratory, the third person is usually expressed by αὐτός in its various forms. Attic poetry, however, frequently uses the older forms.

Personal Pronouns

	1st Person = *I, we*		2nd Person = *you*		3rd Person = *he, she, it, they*	
	Homeric	Attic	Homeric	Attic	Homeric	Attic
Sg. N	ἐγώ [ἐγών]	ἐγώ	σύ	σύ	—	—
G	μεῦ, ἐμεῖο	**(ἐ)μοῦ**	σεῦ, σεῖο	**σοῦ**	ἕο	οὗ
D	(ἐ)μοί	(ἐ)μοί	σοί [τοι]	σοί	οἷ	οἷ
A	(ἐ)μέ	(ἐ)μέ	σέ	σέ	μίν, ἕ	ἕ
Pl. N	ἡμεῖς [ἄμμες]	ἡμεῖς	ὑμεῖς	ὑμεῖς	—	**σφεῖς**
G	ἡμέων	**ἡμῶν**	ὑμέων	**ὑμῶν**	σφέων	**σφῶν**
D	ἡμῖν	ἡμῖν	ὑμῖν	ὑμῖν	σφί(σι) (ν)	σφίσι(ν)
A	ἡμέας, ἄμμε	**ἡμᾶς**	ὑμέας	**ὑμᾶς**	σφέας	**σφᾶς**

In Attic Greek, αὐτός ("himself") is used as a 3rd person pronoun, but not in the nominative:

	(m)	(f)	(n)
Sg.G	αὐτοῦ	αὐτῆς	αὐτοῦ
D	αὐτῷ	αὐτῇ	αὐτῷ
A	αὐτόν	αὐτήν	αὐτό
Pl.G	αὐτῶν	αὐτῶν	αὐτῶν
D	αὐτοῖς	αὐταῖς	αὐτοῖς
A	αὐτούς	αὐτάς	αὐτά

3. τὶς, τὶ, the indefinite pronoun, and τίς, τί, the interrogative pronoun, are the same in form, being distinguished only by the pitch mark. In Attic they are declined regularly on the stem τιν- but have two shortened forms. (See chart below.)

4. ὅστις, ἥτις, ὅ τι, the indefinite relative and indirect interrogative is a combination of the relative pronoun ὅς, ἥ, ὅ and τὶς, τὶ/ τίς, τί. Both parts are declined, except in the shortened forms. ἅττα is an irregular substitute for ἅτινα. (Indirect interrogatives are commonly used in indirect questions.)

Indefinite and Interrogative Pronouns

τὶς, τὶ = *any one*

	Homeric		Attic	
	(m)	(n)	(m)	(n)
Sg.N	τὶς	τὶ	τὶς	τὶ
G	τευ	τευ	**τινός, του**	**τινός, του**
D	τῳ, τεῳ	τῳ, τεῳ	**τινί, τῳ**	**τινί, τῳ**
A	τινά	τὶ	τινά	τὶ
Pl.N	τινές	τινά	τινές	τινά
G	τεων	τεων	**τινῶν**	**τινῶν**
D	τεοισι	τεοισι	**τισί**	**τισί**
A	τίνας	τινά	τινάς	τινά

τίς, τί = *who?*

	Homeric		Attic	
	(m)	(n)	(m)	(n)
Sg.N	τίς	τί	τίς	τί
G	τεῦ	τεῦ	**τίνος, τοῦ**	**τίνος, τοῦ**
D	τῷ, τέῳ	τῷ, τέῳ	**τίνι, τῷ**	**τίνι, τῷ**
A	τινά	τί	τίνα	τί
Pl.N	τίνες	τίνα	τίνες	τίνα
G	τέων	τέων	**τίνων**	**τίνων**
D	τέοισι	τέοισι	**τίσι**	**τίσι**
A	τίνας	τίνα	τίνας	τίνα

Indefinite Relative / Indirect Interrogative

ὅστις, ἥτις, ὅ τι = *whoever, whatever*

	(m)	(f)	(n)
Sg.N	ὅστις	ἥτις	ὅ τι
G	οὕτινος, ὅτου	ἧστινος	οὕτινος, ὅτου
D	ᾧτινι, ὅτῳ	ᾗτινι	ᾧτινι, ὅτῳ
A	ὅντινα	ἥντινα	ὅ τι
Pl.N	οἵτινες	αἵτινες	ἅτινα, ἅττα
G	ὧντινων, ὅτων	ὧντινων	ὧντινων, ὅτων
D	οἷστισι, ὅτοις	αἷστισι	οἷστισι, ὅτοις
A	οὕστινας	ἅστινας	ἅτινα, ἅττα

PART III
CONJUGATION

A. The Regular Verb

(See chart on following pages)

The conjugation of the Attic verb follows almost the same pattern and adds much the same endings as the verb in Homer. Here are all the differences.

1. The most important change to note is that Attic Greek makes a clear distinction between the future middle and the future passive. The special forms of the future passive are made up in this way: aor.-pass.-stem + -ησ- + fut.-mid.-endings.

I shall be loosed	λυθ-ήσ-ομαι
We shall be known	γνωσθ-ησ-όμεθα
They will be seen	ὀφθ-ήσ-ονται

2. Attic Greek, unlike Homeric Greek, uses a future optative. It is formed of the future stem plus the present optative endings.

fut. act. opt.	λύσ-οιμι, λύσ-οις
fut. mid. opt.	λυσ-οίμην, λύσ-οιο
fut. pass. opt.	λυθ-ησ-οίμην, λυθ-ήσ-οιο

3. Contraction takes place:
   (1) in the 2nd person singular of the middle.
   (2) in the 3rd aorist subjunctive.
   (3) in the pluperfect active 1st singular.

4. The longer forms of the infinitives are not used. Note also that the perfect active infinitive ends in -εναι (λελυκέναι).

5. The perfect middle subjunctive and optative use periphrastic (two-part) forms consisting of the perfect middle participle and the subjunctive or optative of εἰμί : e.g., λελυμένος ὦ.

6. The perfect active subjunctive and optative often use periphrastic (two-part) forms consisting of the perfect active participle and the subjunctive or optative of εἰμί : e.g., λελυκὼς ὦ rather than λελύκω.

B. Contract Verbs

(See chart on following pages)

1. The present stem of some verbs and the future stem of a few others end in ε-, α-, or ο-. These vowels ordinarily contract with the initial vowel or diphthong of the verb endings. Since the present and future endings are the same, the contractions will be identical for both tenses.
2. The ordinary rules for contraction, given under General Principles, apply here. However, the infinitive ending -ειν is itself the result of contraction from -εεν and therefore contracts with α to -αν (α+ε+εν=αν), and contracts with ο to -ουν (ο+ε+εν=ουν).

Attic Verb Endings: Active

	Present λυ-	Future λυσ-	1 Aor. λυσ-	2 Aor. ἰδ-	3 Aor. β-	Perfect λελυκ-
Indicative						
1 sg.	-ω	-ω				-α
2 sg.	-εις	-εις				-ας
3 sg.	-ει	-ει				-ε(ν)
1 pl.	-ομεν	-ομεν				-αμεν
2 pl.	-ετε	-ετε				-ατε
3 pl.	-ουσι(ν)	-ουσι(ν)				-ᾱσι(ν)
	(Impf.)					(Plpf.)
1 sg.	-ον		-α	-ον	-ην	**-η**
2 sg.	-ες		-ας	-ες	-ης	-ης
3 sg.	-ε(ν)		-ε(ν)	-ε(ν)	-η	-ει
1 pl.	-ομεν		-αμεν	-ομεν	-ημεν	-εμεν
2 pl.	-ετε		-ατε	-ετε	-ητε	-ετε
3 pl.	-ον		-αν	-ον	-ησαν	-εσαν
Subjunctive						
1 sg.	-ω		-ω	-ω	**-ω**	pf. act. ptc.
2 sg.	-ῃς		-ῃς	-ῃς	**-ῃς**	+ subj. of
3 sg.	-ῃ		-ῃ	-ῃ	**-ῃ**	εἰμί
1 pl.	-ωμεν		-ωμεν	-ωμεν	**-ωμεν**	cf. III.A.6
2 pl.	-ητε		-ητε	-ητε	**-ητε**	
3 pl.	-ωσι(ν)		-ωσι(ν)	-ωσι(ν)	**-ωσι(ν)**	
Optative						
1 sg.	-οιμι	-οιμι	-αιμι	-οιμι	-αιην	pf. act. ptc.
2 sg.	-οις	-οις	-ειας, **-αις**	-οις	-αιης	+ opt. of
3 sg.	-οι	-οι	-ειε(ν), **-αι**	-οι	-αιη	εἰμί
1 pl.	-οιμεν	-οιμεν	-αιμεν	-οιμεν	-αι(η)μεν	cf. III.A.6
2 pl.	-οιτε	-οιτε	-αιτε	-οιτε	-αι(η)τε	
3 pl.	-οιεν	-οιεν	-ειαν, **-αιεν**	-οιεν	-αιεν, **-αιησαν**	
Imperative						
2 sg.	-ε		-ον	-ε	-ηθι	-ε
3 sg.	-ετω		-ατω	-ετω	-ητω	-ετω
2 pl.	-ετε		-ατε	-ετε	-ητε	-ετε
3 pl.	-οντων		-αντων	-οντων	-εντων	-ετωσαν
Infinitive	-ειν	-ειν	-αι	-ειν	-ηναι	**-εναι**
Participle						
m:	-ων	-ων	-ᾱς	-ων	-ᾱς	-ως
f:	-ουσα	-ουσα	-ᾱσα	-ουσα	-ᾱσα	-υια
n:	-ον	-ον	-αν	-ον	-αν	-ος

(<u>Note</u> on 3 aor.: some verbs have ω or ῡ in place of η, and οι or υι in place of αι. Besides the endings listed above, 3 aor. participles also show the following endings: -ους, -ουσα, -ον / -ῡς, -ῦσα, -υν)

Attic Verb Endings: Middle and Passive

	Middle Passive		Middle Only			Passive Only	
	Present M.P. λυ-	Perfect M.P. λελυ-	1 Aor. M. λυσ-	2 Aor. M. ἰδ-	Future M. λυσ-	Future P. λυθ-ησ-	Aorist P. λυθ-
Indicative							
1 sg.	-ομαι	-μαι				-ομαι	-ομαι
2 sg.	**-ῃ, -ει**	-σαι				**-ῃ, -ει**	**-ῃ, -ει**
3 sg.	-εται	-ται				-εται	-εται
1 pl.	-ομεθα	-μεθα				-ομεθα	-ομεθα
2 pl.	-εσθε	-σθε				-εσθε	-εσθε
3 pl.	-ονται	-νται				-ονται	-ονται
	(Impf.)	(Plpf.)					
1 sg.	-ομην	-μην	-αμην	-ομην			-ην
2 sg.	**-ου**	-σο	**-ω**	**-ου**			-ης
3 sg.	-ετο	-το	-ατο	-ετο			-η
1 pl.	-ομεθα	-μεθα	-αμεθα	-ομεθα			-ημεν
2 pl.	-εσθε	-σθε	-ασθε	-εσθε			-ητε
3 pl.	-οντο	-ντο	-αντο	-οντο			-ησαν
Subjunctive							
1 sg.	-ωμαι	pf. mid. ptc. + subj. of εἰμί cf. III.A.5	-ωμαι	-ωμαι			-ῶ
2 sg.	**-ῃ**		**-ῃ**	**-ῃ**			-ῇς
3 sg.	-ηται		-ηται	-ηται			-ῇ
1 pl.	-ωμεθα		-ωμεθα	-ωμεθα			-ῶμεν
2 pl.	-ησθε		-ησθε	-ησθε			-ῆτε
3 pl.	-ωνται		-ωνται	-ωνται			-ῶσι(ν)
Optative							
1 sg.	-οιμην	pf. mid. ptc. + opt. of εἰμί cf. III.A.5	-αιμην	-οιμην	**-οιμην**	**-οιμην**	-ειην
2 sg.	-οιο		-αιο	-οιο	**-οιο**	**-οιο**	-ειης
3 sg.	-οιτο		-αιτο	-οιτο	**-οιτο**	**-οιτο**	-ειη
1 pl.	-οιμεθα		-αιμεθα	-οιμεθα	**-οιμεθα**	**-οιμεθα**	-ει(η)μεν
2 pl.	-οισθε		-αισθε	-οισθε	**-οισθε**	**-οισθε**	-ει(η)τε
3 pl.	-οιντο		-αιντο	-οιντο	**-οιντο**	**-οιντο**	-ειησαν/-ειεν
Imperative							
2 sg.	**-ου**	-σο	-αι	**-ου**			-ηθι
3 sg.	-εσθω	-σθω	-ασθω	-εσθω			-ητω
2 pl.	-εσθε	-σθε	-ασθε	-εσθε			-ητε
3 pl.	-εσθων	-σθων	-ασθων	-εσθων			-εντων
Infinitive	-εσθαι	-σθαι	-ασθαι	-εσθαι	-εσθαι	-εσθαι	-ηναι
Participle							
m:	-ομενος	-μενος	-αμενος	-ομενος	-ομενος	-ομενος	-εις
f:	-ομενη	-μενη	-αμενη	-ομενη	-ομενη	-ομενη	-εισα
n:	-ομενον	-μενον	-αμενον	-ομενον	-ομενον	-ομενον	-εν

Contract Verbs

This table lists for easy reference all the possible contracted verb endings in the present system. Since the endings of the future are the same as the present endings, the contractions also will be the same. The stem vowel in parentheses contracts with the regular endings to give the forms arranged below it.

	Pres. Act. τιμάω τιμ-(α)	Pres. Mid. τιμάομαι τιμ-(α)	Pres. Act. φιλέω φιλ-(ε)	Pres. Mid. φιλέομαι φιλ-(ε)	Pres. Act. δηλόω δηλ-(ο)	Pres. Mid. δηλόομαι δηλ-(ο)
Indicative						
1 sg.	-ῶ	-ῶμαι	-ῶ	-οῦμαι	-ῶ	-οῦμαι
2 sg.	-ᾷς	-ᾷ	-εῖς	-εῖ, -ῇ	-οῖς	-οῖ
3 sg.	-ᾷ	-ᾶται	-εῖ	-εῖται	-οῖ	-οῦται
1 pl.	-ῶμεν	-ώμεθα	-οῦμεν	-ούμεθα	-οῦμεν	-ούμεθα
2 pl.	-ᾶτε	-ᾶσθε	-εῖτε	-εῖσθε	-οῦτε	-οῦσθε
3 pl.	-ῶσι	-ῶνται	-οῦσι	-οῦνται	-οῦσι	-οῦνται
	(Impf.)	(Impf.)	(Impf.)	(Impf.)	(Impf.)	(Impf.)
1 sg.	-ων	-ώμην	-ουν	-ούμην	-ουν	-ούμην
2 sg.	-ᾶς	-ῶ	-εις	-οῦ	-ους	-οῦ
3 sg.	-ᾶ	-ᾶτο	-ει	-εῖτο	-ου	-οῦτο
1 pl.	-ῶμεν	-ώμεθα	-οῦμεν	-ούμεθα	-οῦμεν	-ούμεθα
2 pl.	-ᾶτε	-ᾶσθε	-εῖτε	-εῖσθε	-οῦτε	-οῦσθε
3 pl.	-ων	-ῶντο	-ουν	-οῦντο	-ουν	-οῦντο
Subjunctive						
1 sg.	-ῶ	-ῶμαι	-ῶ	-ῶμαι	-ῶ	-ῶμαι
2 sg.	-ᾷς	-ᾷ	-ῇς	-ῇ	-οῖς	-οῖ
3 sg.	-ᾷ	-ᾶται	-ῇ	-ῆται	-οῖ	-ῶται
1 pl.	-ῶμεν	-ώμεθα	-ῶμεν	-ώμεθα	-ῶμεν	-ώμεθα
2 pl.	-ᾶτε	-ᾶσθε	-ῆτε	-ῆσθε	-ῶτε	-ῶσθε
3 pl.	-ῶσι	-ῶνται	-ῶσι	-ῶνται	-ῶσι	-ῶνται
Optative						
1 sg.	-ῴην	-ῴμην	-οίην	-οίμην	-οίην	-οίμην
2 sg.	-ῴης	-ῷο	-οίης	-οῖο	-οίης	-οῖο
3 sg.	-ῴη	-ῷτο	-οίη	-οῖτο	-οίη	-οῖτο
1 pl.	-ῷμεν	-ῴμεθα	-οῖμεν	-οίμεθα	-οῖμεν	-οίμεθα
2 pl.	-ῷτε	-ῷσθε	-οῖτε	-οῖσθε	-οῖτε	-οῖσθε
3 pl.	-ῷεν	-ῷντο	-οῖεν	-οῖντο	-οῖεν	-οῖντο
Imperative						
2 sg.	-α	-ω	-ει	-ου	-ου	-ου
3 sg.	-άτω	-άσθω	-είτω	-είσθω	-ούτω	-ούσθω
2 pl.	-ᾶτε	-ᾶσθε	-εῖτε	-εῖσθε	-οῦτε	-οῦσθε
3 pl.	-ώντων	-άσθων	-ούντων	-είσθων	-ούντων	-ούσθων
Infinitive						
	-ᾶν	-ᾶσθαι	-εῖν	-εῖσθαι	-οῦν	-οῦσθαι
Participle						
m:	-ῶν	-ώμενος	-ῶν	-ούμενος	-ῶν	-ούμενος
f:	-ῶσα	-ωμένη	-οῦσα	-ουμένη	-οῦσα	-ουμένη
n:	-ῶν	-ώμενον	-οῦν	-ούμενον	-οῦν	-ούμενον

C. -MI Verbs

As you already know, the vast majority of Greek verbs belong to a single conjugation. However, approximately 77 verbs (in the whole of Greek literature), though following the regular conjugation in most of their forms, have certain peculiarities in common. They are called -μι verbs because the first principal part (active) ends in -μι, or "non-thematic" verbs because both active and deponent verbs of this type add the verb-endings without the "thematic" vowel (for example, δύνα-μαι *I can*, instead of δυνά-ομαι). Thus -μι verbs are easily recognized from the first principal part.

How are -μι verbs conjugated? 36 of them follow δείκνῡμι; 25 others follow ἵστημι. The other 16 are similarly conjugated but have certain irregularities of their own and must be learned individually. However, of these 16 verbs, 9 are so rare that it is not likely you will ever meet them, thus leaving only 7 that need be studied. You have already had some acquaintance with them. They are:

τίθημι	*I place*	φημί	*I say*
δίδωμι	*I give*	εἰμί	*I am*
ἵημι	*I send*	εἶμι	*I shall go*
		ἧμαι	*I sit* (usually κάθ-ημαι in Attic)

δείκνῡμι *I show*, and ἵστημι *I put*

(See chart on following page)

These two verbs, which are the models for all the ordinary -μι verbs, are much alike.

1. They are irregular only in the present system.
2. The middle has regular endings but drops the thematic vowel.
3. The stem vowel is shortened except in the act. ind. sg. and impt. sg.

Note: Even in the present system some regular forms are found.
δείκνῡμι takes regular endings in the subj. and opt., act. and mid.
ἵστημι takes regular act. and mid. subj. endings (which absorb the stem vowel).

D. Irregular -MI Verbs

φημί *I say*

(See chart on following page)

φημί is not used in the middle in Attic Greek although it is in Homer. It is conjugated as ἵστημι except: (1) impt. sg. = φα-θί or φά-θι. (2) φή-ς is sometimes written φῄ-ς.

κάθημαι *I sit*

(See chart on following page)

The deponent verb ἧμαι is usually found in its compound form, κάθημαι in Attic, and in fact is often augmented as a simple verb, e.g., ἐκαθήμην. It takes middle endings without the thematic vowel except in the subj. and opt., where the regular endings are added and absorb the stem vowel.

	-MI Verbs			Irregular -MI Verbs		
	δείκνυ-μι Pres. Act.	ἵστη-μι Pres. Act.	δείκνυ-μαι Pres. Mid.	ἵστα-μαι Pres. Mid.	φη-μί Pres. Act. (No middle)	κάθ-ημαι Pres. Mid. (Deponent)
Indicative						
1 sg.	δείκνῡ-μι	ἵστη-μι	δείκνυ-μαι	ἵστα-μαι	φη-μί	κάθη-μαι
2 sg.	δείκνῡ-ς	ἵστη-ς	δείκνυ-σαι	ἵστα-σαι	φή-ς[4]	κάθη-σαι
3 sg.	δείκνῡ-σι	ἵστη-σι	δείκνυ-ται	ἵστα-ται	φη-σί	κάθη-ται
1 pl.	δείκνυ-μεν	ἵστα-μεν	δεικνύ-μεθα	ἱστά-μεθα	φα-μέν	καθή-μεθα
2 pl.	δείκνυ-τε	ἵστα-τε	δείκνυ-σθε	ἵστα-σθε	φα-τέ	κάθη-σθε
3 pl.	δεικνύ-ᾱσι	ἱστᾶσι[2]	δείκνυ-νται	ἵστα-νται	φᾶ-σι[5]	κάθη-νται
	(Impf.)	(Impf.)	(Impf.)	(Impf.)	(Impf.)	(Impf.)
1 sg.	ἐδείκνῡ-ν	ἵστη-ν	ἐδεικνύ-μην	ἱστά-μην	ἔφη-ν	ἐκαθή-μην
2 sg.	ἐδείκνῡ-ς	ἵστη-ς	ἐδείκνυ-σο	ἵστα-σο	ἔφη-ς[6]	ἐκάθη-σο
3 sg.	ἐδείκνῡ	ἵστη	ἐδείκνυ-το	ἵστα-το	ἔφη	ἐκάθη-το
1 pl.	ἐδείκνυ-μεν	ἵστα-μεν	ἐδεικνύ-μεθα	ἱστά-μεθα	ἔφα-μεν	ἐκαθή-μεθα
2 pl.	ἐδείκνυ-τε	ἵστα-τε	ἐδείκνυ-σθε	ἵστα-σθε	ἔφα-τε	ἐκάθη-σθε
3 pl.	ἐδείκνυ-σαν	ἵστα-σαν	ἐδείκνυ-ντο	ἵστα-ντο	ἔφα-σαν	ἐκάθη-ντο
Subjunctive						
1 sg.	δεικνύ-ω	ἱστ-ῶ	δεικνύ-ωμαι	ἱστ-ῶμαι	φ-ῶ	καθ-ῶμαι
2 sg.	δεικνύ-ῃς	ἱστ-ῇς	δεικνύ-ῃ	ἱστ-ῇ	φ-ῇς	καθ-ῇ
3 sg.	δεικνύ-ῃ	ἱστ-ῇ	δεικνύ-ηται	ἱστ-ῆται	φ-ῇ	καθ-ῆται
1 pl.	δεικνύ-ωμεν	ἱστ-ῶμεν	δεικνυ-ώμεθα	ἱστ-ώμεθα	φ-ῶμεν	καθ-ώμεθα
2 pl.	δεικνύ-ητε	ἱστ-ῆτε	δεικνύ-ησθε	ἱστ-ῆσθε	φ-ῆτε	καθ-ῆσθε
3 pl.	δεικνύ-ωσι	ἱστ-ῶσι	δεικνύ-ωνται	ἱστ-ῶνται	φ-ῶσι	καθ-ῶνται
Optative						
1 sg.	δεικνύ-οιμι	ἱσταίην[3]	δεικνυ-οίμην	ἱσταίμην	φαίην	καθ-οίμην
2 sg.	δεικνύ-οις	ἱσταίης	δεικνύ-οιο	ἱσταῖο	φαίης	καθ-οῖο
3 sg.	δεικνύ-οι	ἱσταίη	δεικνύ-οιτο	ἱσταῖτο	φαίη	καθ-οῖτο
1 pl.	δεικνύ-οιμεν	ἱσταίημεν	δεικνυ-οίμεθα	ἱσταίμεθα	φαίημεν	καθ-οίμεθα
2 pl.	δεικνύ-οιτε	ἱσταίητε	δεικνύ-οισθε	ἱσταῖσθε	φαίητε	καθ-οῖσθε
3 pl.	δεικνύ-οιεν	ἱσταίησαν	δεικνύ-οιντο	ἱσταῖντο	φαίησαν	καθ-οῖντο
		contracted:			contracted:	
1 pl.		ἱσταῖμεν			φαῖμεν	
2 pl.		ἱσταῖτε			φαῖτε	
3 pl.		ἱσταῖεν			φαῖεν	
Imperative						
2 sg.	δείκνῡ	ἵστη	δείκνυ-σο	ἵστα-σο	φά-θι	κάθη-σο
3 sg.	δεικνύ-τω	ἱστά-τω	δεικνύ-σθω	ἱστά-σθω	φά-τω	καθή-σθω
2 pl.	δείκνυ-τε	ἵστα-τε	δείκνυ-σθε	ἵστα-σθε	φά-τε	κάθη-σθε
3 pl.	δεικνύ-ντων	ἱστά-ντων	δεικνύ-σθων	ἱστά-σθων	φά-ντων	καθή-σθων
Infinitive						
	δεικνύ-ναι	ἱστά-ναι	δείκνυ-σθαι	ἵστα-σθαι	φά-ναι	καθῆ-σθαι
Participle						
m:	δεικνῡ́ς[1]	ἱστάς[1]	δεικνύ-μενος	ἱστά-μενος	φάς[1]	καθή-μενος
f:	δεικνῦσα	ἱστᾶσα	δεικνυ-μένη	ἱστα-μένη	φᾶσα	καθη-μένη
n:	δεικνύν	ἱστάν	δεικνύ-μενον	ἱστά-μενον	φάν	καθή-μενον

[1] Compensative lengthening.
[2] Contraction of ἱστά-ασι.
[3] Compare 3rd aor. act.
[4] Also written φής.
[5] Contraction of φά-ασι.
[6] Sometimes ἔφησθα.

εἰμί *I am*

εἰμί has the stem ἐσ- which frequently drops the σ and then undergoes various changes— some regular (like the contraction of the subj. and ptc., and the augment of the impf.), others irregular. The future ἔσομαι is regular except for the shortened 3rd person sg., ἔσται. The forms in bold type are those that are new to you.

	Ind. Pres.	Ind. Impf.	Subj. Pres.	Opt. Pres.	Impt. Pres.
1 sg.	εἰμί	**ἦ or ἦν**	ὦ	εἴην	
2 sg.	**εἶ**	ἦσθα	ᾖς	εἴης	**ἴσθι**
3 sg.	ἐστί	ἦν	ᾖ	εἴη	**ἔστω**
1 pl.	**ἐσμέν**	ἦμεν	ὦμεν	εἴημεν/εἶμεν	
2 pl.	ἐστέ	ἦτε	ἦτε	εἴητε/εἶτε	**ἔστε**
3 pl.	εἰσί	ἦσαν	ὦσι	εἴησαν/εἶεν	**ἔστων**

INF. PRES.   εἶναι
PTC. PRES. (m.f.n.)   **ὤν, οὖσα, ὄν** (gen. ὄντος, οὔσης, ὄντος)

εἶμι *I shall go*

εἶμι is present in form but in the present indicative has future meaning. It is usually used in Attic as the future of ἔρχομαι *I come, I go.* (Notice that its first two forms are the same as those of εἰμί *I am.*) There are two stems: εἰ- (augmented regularly) and ἰ-. The subj., opt., and ptc. are regular. Recall that you have already learned in the Homer course the inf., ptc., and pres. ind. 3 sg.

	Ind. Pres.	Ind. Impf.	Subj. Pres.	Opt. Pres.	Impt. Pres.
1 sg.	εἶ-μι	ᾖ-α/ᾔειν	ἴ-ω	ἴ-οιμι/ἰοίην	
2 sg.	εἶ	ᾔ-εις/ᾔεισθα	ἴ-ῃς	ἴ-οις	ἴ-θι
3 sg.	εἶ-σι	ᾔ-ει/ᾔειν	ἴ-ῃ	ἴ-οι	ἴτω
1 pl.	ἴ-μεν	ᾖ-μεν	ἴ-ωμεν	ἴ-οιμεν	
2 pl.	ἴ-τε	ᾖ-τε	ἴ-ητε	ἴ-οιτε	ἴ-τε
3 pl.	ἴ-ᾱσι	ᾖ-σαν/ᾔεσαν	ἴ-ωσι	ἴ-οιεν	ἰόντων

INF. PRES.   ἰ-έναι
PTC. PRES. (m.f.n.)   ἰ-ών, ἰ-οῦσα, ἰ-όν (gen. ἰόντος, ἰούσης, ἰόντος)

ἵημι *I send,* τίθημι *I place,* δίδωμι *I give*

(See chart on following pages)

These verbs are very much like ἵστημι. They differ in two main respects:

     1. The act. impt. sg. and most of the impf. act. sg. take regular endings and then contract.

     2. These three verbs are irregular also in the **2nd aorist**. 1st aorist forms are used only in the act. ind. sg.

Notice that the 2nd aorist is the same as the present but drops the so-called "present reduplication," that is, the iota plus the initial consonant. Thus τιθῶ becomes θῶ, διδοίην becomes δοίην. The 2nd aorist, however, does differ from the present in these three places:

     1. act. impt. sg. takes -ς, not -ε.

     2. act. inf. lengthens.

     3. mid. impf. and impt. contract in the 2nd sg.

ἵημι, τίθημι, δίδωμι
  Active

	Present System			2nd Aorist System		
	ἵημι	τίθημι	δίδωμι	ἵημι	τίθημι	δίδωμι
	ἱη-, ἱε-	τιθη-, τιθε-	διδω-, διδο-	ἑ-	θε-	δο-
Indicative						
1 sg.	ἵη-μι	τίθη-μι	δίδω-μι	(Note: ἑ- is augmented to εἱ-.)		
2 sg.	ἵη-ς	τίθη-ς	δίδω-ς			
3 sg.	ἵη-σι	τίθη-σι	δίδω-σι			
1 pl.	ἵε-μεν	τίθε-μεν	δίδο-μεν			
2 pl.	ἵε-τε	τίθε-τε	δίδο-τε			
3 pl.	ἱᾶσι	§τιθέ-ᾱσι	§ διδό-ᾱσι			
	(Impf.)	(Impf.)	(Impf.)			
1 sg.	ἵη-ν	ἐτίθη-ν	§ ἐδίδουν	# ἧκα	# ἔθηκα	# ἔδωκα
2 sg.	§ ἵεις	§ ἐτίθεις	§ ἐδίδους	# ἧκας	# ἔθηκας	# ἔδωκας
3 sg.	§ ἵει	§ ἐτίθει	§ ἐδίδου	# ἧκε	# ἔθηκε	# ἔδωκε
1 pl.	ἵε-μεν	ἐτίθε-μεν	ἐδίδο-μεν	εἷ-μεν	ἔθε-μεν	ἔδο-μεν
2 pl.	ἵε-τε	ἐτίθε-τε	ἐδίδο-τε	εἷ-τε	ἔθε-τε	ἔδο-τε
3 pl.	ἵε-σαν	ἐτίθε-σαν	ἐδίδο-σαν	εἷ-σαν	ἔθε-σαν	ἔδο-σαν
Subjunctive						
1 sg.	ἱ-ῶ	τιθ-ῶ	διδ-ῶ [1]	ὦ	θ-ῶ	δ-ῶ [1]
2 sg.	ἱ-ῇς	τιθ-ῇς	διδ-ῷς	ᾖς	θ-ῇς	δ-ῷς
3 sg.	ἱ-ῇ	τιθ-ῇ	διδ-ῷ	ᾖ	θ-ῇ	δ-ῷ
1 pl.	ἱ-ῶμεν	τιθ-ῶμεν	διδ-ῶμεν	ὦμεν	θ-ῶμεν	δ-ῶμεν
2 pl.	ἱ-ῆτε	τιθ-ῆτε	διδ-ῶτε	ἦτε	θ-ῆτε	δ-ῶτε
3 pl.	ἱ-ῶσι	τιθ-ῶσι	διδ-ῶσι	ὦσι	θ-ῶσι	δ-ῶσι
Optative						
1 sg.	ἱε-ίην	τιθε-ίην	διδο-ίην	ἑ-ίην	θε-ίην	δο-ίην
2 sg.	ἱε-ίης	τιθε-ίης	διδο-ίης	ἑ-ίης	θε-ίης	δο-ίης
3 sg.	ἱε-ίη	τιθε-ίη	διδο-ίη	ἑ-ίη	θε-ίη	δο-ίη
1 pl.	ἱε-ίημεν	τιθε-ίημεν	διδο-ίημεν	ἑ-ίημεν	θε-ίημεν	δο-ίημεν
2 pl.	ἱε-ίητε	τιθε-ίητε	διδο-ίητε	ἑ-ίητε	θε-ίητε	δο-ίητε
3 pl.	ἱε-ίησαν	τιθε-ίησαν	διδο-ίησαν	ἑ-ίησαν	θε-ίησαν	δο-ίησαν
	contracted:	contracted:	contracted:	contracted:	contracted:	contracted:
1 pl.	ἱεῖμεν	τιθεῖμεν	διδοῖμεν	εἷμεν	θεῖμεν	δοῖμεν
2 pl.	ἱεῖτε	τιθεῖτε	διδοῖτε	εἷτε	θεῖτε	δοῖτε
3 pl.	ἱεῖεν	τιθεῖεν	διδοῖεν	εἷεν	θεῖεν	δοῖεν
Imperative						
2 sg.	§ ἵει	§ τίθει	§ δίδου	ἕ-ς	θέ-ς	δό-ς
3 sg.	ἱέ-τω	τιθέ-τω	διδό-τω	ἕ-τω	θέ-τω	δό-τω
2 pl.	ἵε-τε	τίθε-τε	δίδο-τε	ἕ-τε	θέ-τε	δό-τε
3 pl.	ἱέ-ντων	τιθέ-ντων	διδό-ντων	ἕ-ντων	θέ-ντων	δό-ντων
Infinitive						
	ἱέ-ναι	τιθέ-ναι	διδό-ναι	εἷναι	θεῖναι	δοῦναι
Participle						
m:	ἱείς	τιθείς	διδούς	εἵς	θείς	δούς
f:	ἱεῖσα	τιθεῖσα	διδοῦσα	εἷσα	θεῖσα	δοῦσα
n:	ἱέν	τιθέν	διδόν	ἕν	θέν	δόν

§ These forms do not follow ἵστημι.   # These irregular 1st aor. forms are used in the ind. sg.   [1] Contract according to rule.

ἵημι, τίθημι, δίδωμι
Middle Passive

	Present System			2nd Aorist System (Middle Only)		
	ἵημι	τιθημι	διδωμι	ἵημι	τιθημι	διδωμι
	ἱε-	τιθε-	διδο-	ἑ-	θε-	δο-
Indicative						
1 sg.	ἵε-μαι	τίθε-μαι	δίδο-μαι	(Note: ἑ- is augmented to εἱ-.)		
2 sg.	ἵε-σαι	τίθε-σαι	δίδο-σαι			
3 sg.	ἵε-ται	τίθε-ται	δίδο-ται			
1 pl.	ἱέ-μεθα	τιθέ-μεθα	διδό-μεθα			
2 pl.	ἵε-σθε	τίθε-σθε	δίδο-σθε			
3 pl.	ἵε-νται	τίθε-νται	δίδο-νται			
	(Impf.)	(Impf.)	(Impf.)			
1 sg.	ἱέ-μην	ἐτιθέ-μην	ἐδιδό-μην	εἵ-μην	ἐθέ-μην	ἐδό-μην
2 sg.	ἵε-σο	ἐτίθε-σο	ἐδίδο-σο	εἵ-σο	# ἔθου	# ἔδου
3 sg.	ἵε-το	ἐτίθε-το	ἐδίδο-το	εἵ-το	ἔθε-το	ἔδο-το
1 pl.	ἱέ-μεθα	ἐτιθέ-μεθα	ἐδιδό-μεθα	εἵ-μεθα	ἐθέ-μεθα	ἐδό-μεθα
2 pl.	ἵε-σθε	ἐτίθε-σθε	ἐδίδο-σθε	εἵ-σθε	ἔθε-σθε	ἔδο-σθε
3 pl.	ἵε-ντο	ἐτίθε-ντο	ἐδιδό-ντο	εἵ-ντο	ἔθε-ντο	ἔδο-ντο
Subjunctive						
1 sg.	ἱ-ῶμαι	τιθ-ῶμαι	διδ-ῶμαι [1]	ὦμαι	θ-ῶμαι	δ-ῶμαι [1]
2 sg.	ἱ-ῇ	τιθ-ῇ	διδ-ῷ	ἧ	θ-ῇ	δ-ῷ
3 sg.	ἱ-ῆται	τιθ-ῆται	διδ-ῶται	ἧται	θ-ῆται	δ-ῶται
1 pl.	ἱ-ώμεθα	τιθ-ώμεθα	διδ-ώμεθα	ὥμεθα	θ-ώμεθα	δ-ώμεθα
2 pl.	ἱ-ῆσθε	τιθ-ῆσθε	διδ-ῶσθε	ἧσθε	θ-ῆσθε	δ-ῶσθε
3 pl.	ἱ-ῶνται	τιθ-ῶνται	διδ-ῶνται	ὦνται	θ-ῶνται	δ-ῶνται
Optative						
1 sg.	ἱείμην	τιθείμην	διδοίμην	εἵμην	θείμην	δοίμην
2 sg.	ἱεῖο	τιθεῖο	διδοῖο	εἷο	θεῖο	δοῖο
3 sg.	ἱεῖτο	τιθεῖτο	διδοῖτο	εἷτο	θεῖτο	δοῖτο
1 pl.	ἱείμεθα	τιθείμεθα	διδοίμεθα	εἵμεθα	θείμεθα	δοίμεθα
2 pl.	ἱεῖσθε	τιθεῖσθε	διδοῖσθε	εἷσθε	θεῖσθε	δοῖσθε
3 pl.	ἱεῖντο	τιθεῖντο	διδοῖντο	εἷντο	θεῖντο	δοῖντο
Imperative						
2 sg.	ἵε-σο	τίθε-σο	δίδο-σο	# οὗ	# θοῦ	# δοῦ
3 sg.	ἵετο	τιθέ-σθω	διδό-σθω	ἔ-σθω	θέ-σθω	δό-σθω
2 pl.	ἵε-σθε	τίθε-σθε	δίδο-σθε	ἔ-σθε	θέ-σθε	δό-σθε
3 pl.	ἵεντο	τιθέ-σθων	διδό-σθων	ἔ-σθων	θέ-σθων	δό-σθων
Infinitive						
	ἵε-σθαι	τίθε-σθαι	δίδο-σθαι	ἔ-σθαι	θέ-σθαι	δό-σθαι
Participle						
m:	ἱέ-μενος	τιθέ-μενος	διδό-μενος	ἔ-μενος	θέ-μενος	δό-μενος
f:	ἱε-μένη	τιθε-μένη	διδο-μένη	ἑ-μένη	θε-μένη	δο-μένη
n:	ἱέ-μενον	τιθέ-μενον	διδό-μενον	ἔ-μενον	θέ-μενον	δό-μενον

[1] Contract according to rule.
These 2nd aor. forms do not follow the present system form.

E. οἶδα *I know*

This irregular verb is not a -μι verb; it uses three different stems and follows no recognizable system. It is classified as a perfect in form but is present and imperfect in meaning. The forms in bold type are those that differ from the Homeric forms you have already learned.

	Ind. Pf. (pres. meaning)	Ind. Ppf. (impf. meaning)	Subj. Pf.	Opt. Pf.	Impt. Pf.
1 sg.	οἶδα	ᾔδη/ᾔδειν	εἰδῶ	εἰδείην	
2 sg.	οἶσθα	ᾔδησθα/ᾔδεισθα	εἰδῇς	εἰδείης	ἴσθι
3 sg.	οἶδε	ᾔδει(ν)	εἰδῇ	εἰδείη	ἴστω
1 pl.	**ἴσμεν**	ᾖσμεν	εἰδῶμεν	εἰδεῖμεν	
2 pl.	ἴστε	ᾖστε	εἰδῆτε	εἰδεῖτε	ἴστε
3 pl.	ἴσασι	ᾖσαν/ᾔδεσαν	εἰδῶσι	εἰδεῖεν	ἴστων

INF. PF.   **εἰδέναι**

PTC. PF. (m.f.n.)   εἰδώς, εἰδυῖα, εἰδός (gen. εἰδότος, εἰδυίας, εἰδότος)

F. Verbs with "Irregular" Principal Parts

In the course of your further study of Greek you will sometimes hear verbs like γιγνώσκω or ὁράω referred to as "irregular" verbs. They are so called because their principal parts change too radically to be predicted from the present, and consequently puzzle the student who has learned the verb by the method of building the whole verb on the present stem or by the method of simple analogy, that is, by constant comparison with a model verb.

From your point of view these "irregular" verbs are quite regular. You are accustomed to basing the entire verb on the principal parts, and know exactly what stem to use for any possible form and how to get that stem. By learning the endings according to systems, you have a clear picture of precisely what endings can be joined to a given stem. Thus you are in a position to build at once any desired form of any verb whose principal parts you know, no matter how odd they may look. Of course, you will have to memorize the principal parts of such "irregular" verbs just as everyone else does, but granted the principal parts (which can always be found in Grammar or Dictionary), you will have no further trouble.

Part IV
SYNTAX

Syntax is here treated under five headings:

    A. The Definite Article
    B. The Relative Pronoun
    C. Syntax of the Noun
    D. Syntax of the Verb by Constructions
    E. Syntax of the Verb by Moods

A. The Definite Article

In Homer ὁ, ἡ, τό was a weak demonstrative pronoun or adjective. In Attic Greek it became so unemphatic as to be nearly equivalent to the English definite article, <u>the</u>, and is usually translated as such in English. Note the following points.

1. The original, Homeric, force of ὁ, ἡ, τό is still sometimes apparent in Attic, especially when used in combination with δέ. For example:

ὁ μὲν . . . ὁ δέ	the one . . . the other
πρὸ τοῦ	before this
ὁ δέ	but he

2. It is sometimes used in Attic prose contrary to the English usage.

    a. Predicate nouns do not take the article, even where the English uses it, unless for some special reason.

πάντων μέτρον ἄνθρωπός ἐστιν.	Man is the measure of all things.
θεὸς ἦν ὁ λόγος	The Word was God.

    b. Proper nouns sometimes take the article to indicate that the person is well known.

ὁ Σωκράτης	Socrates
αἱ τοῦ Ὀδυσσέως νῆες	the boats of Odysseus

    c. Abstract nouns often take the article.

ἀεὶ φιλεῖτε τὴν ἀλήθειαν.	Always love truth.

    d. Possessive pronouns may take the article when modifying a noun referring to a definite thing.

τὸ ἐμὸν ξίφος	my sword (I have a definite one in mind)
ἐμὸν ξίφος	a sword of mine (any one of several)

    e. The article sometimes takes the place of an unemphatic possessive pronoun when the meaning is clear.

πάντα εἶπε τοῖς ἑταίροις.	He told his comrades everything.

    f. The infinitive used as a noun may take the neuter article.

παισὶ τὸ πείθεσθαι τοῦ κελεύειν ἄρειόν ἐστιν.	Obedience is better for children than commanding.

3. By means of the article, a noun in the genitive, an adverb, a prepositional phrase, etc., can be used like an adjective to qualify a noun.

οἱ Ὀδυσσέως ἑταῖροι	the companions of Odysseus
οἱ νῦν (ἄνδρες)	the men of today (The noun may be omitted.)
οἱ παρὰ ἄνακτος ἄγγελοι	the messengers from the king

4. The position of the article is important.

   a. **Attributive position**: an article immediately preceding a qualifying expression is said to put the expression in the attributive position. This is the ordinary position and has no special significance.

   ὁ σοφὸς ἀνήρ *or* ὁ ἀνὴρ ὁ σοφός   the wise man

   b. **Predicate position**: an article following a qualifying expression or separated from it by intervening words is said to put the expression in the predicate position. This position gives emphasis and is frequently equivalent to a clause.

   σοφὸς ὁ ἀνήρ. *or* ὁ ἀνὴρ σοφός.   The man is wise.

   c. The demonstrative adjectives οὗτος, ὅδε, and ἐκεῖνος take the predicate position in Attic prose.

   οὗτος ὁ ἀνήρ *or* ὁ ἀνὴρ οὗτος   this man

   d. αὐτός in the attributive position means *same*; in the predicate position, *self*.

   ὁ αὐτὸς ἀνήρ   the same man
   ὁ ἀνὴρ αὐτός *or* αὐτὸς ὁ ἀνήρ   the man himself

B. The Relative Pronoun

The general rule for all relative pronouns is that they agree with their antecedents in gender and number but their case depends on the construction of their own clause. However, in Attic Greek two peculiar uses must be noted.

1. **Assimilation**: a relative pronoun in the accusative case is sometimes assimilated to the case of its antecedent, provided that this antecedent is itself in the genitive or dative.

   πρὸ τῶν κακῶν ἃ οἶδα (instead of the evils which I know)
   may be written: πρὸ τῶν κακῶν ὧν οἶδα

   αἰνῶ σε ἐπὶ τούτοις ἃ λέγεις (I praise you for these things which you say)
   may be written: αἰνῶ σε ἐπὶ τούτοις οἷς λέγεις. Moreover, the pronominal antecedent may be dropped, as in English: αἰνῶ σε ἐφ' οἷς λέγεις (I praise you for what you say.)

   καλλίστη ἐστι πασῶν ἃς ἑώρακα (She is the most beautiful of all the women whom I have seen)
   may be written: καλλίστη ἐστι πασῶν ὧν ἑώρακα.

2. **Attraction**: the opposite of assimilation is called attraction. The antecedent is sometimes attracted to the relative clause and takes the case of the relative pronoun. (Recall Virgil's use: "urbem, quam statuo, vestra est" instead of the ordinary "urbs, quam statuo, vestra est"— the city which I am founding is yours.)

   αἱ γυναῖκες ἃς ὁρᾷς ἔρχονται (The women whom you see are coming)
   may be written: τὰς γυναῖκας ἃς ὁρᾷς ἔρχονται.

   ὁ ἀνὴρ οὗτος, ὃν ἐζητεῖτε, ἐνθάδε ἐστίν. (This man, whom you were seeking, is here)
   may be written: τὸν ἄνδρα τοῦτον, ὃν ἐζητεῖτε, ἐνθάδε ἐστίν.

C. Syntax of the Noun

Note: the numbers starred contain data not met in Homer or different from Homeric usage. Where the rule is the same as in Homeric Greek, only a reference is given to the relevant section in the *Reading Course in Homeric Greek*.

I. Nominative

1. **Case of the subject** of a finite verb, or of a predicate noun, adjective, or participle agreeing with the subject. (In Attic a neuter plural subject practically always takes a singular verb. §53)

*2. **Nominative with infinitive**: in Greek, unlike Latin, the subject of the infinitive after a main verb of saying, thinking, etc., is not necessarily in the accusative. When the subject of the infinitive is the same as that of the main verb, it is omitted but is considered to be in the nominative. Hence any modifiers will remain in the nominative case.

οἶμαι γνῶναι.	I think I know.
ἔφη εἶναι κρατερός.	He said he was strong.
ἐνομίσατε ἔσεσθαι ὄλβιοι.	You thought you would be happy.

II. Genitive

1. **Case expressing** basic meanings *of*; *from*.
2. **Genitive of comparison**: §18.
3. **Agency**: personal agency is regularly expressed in Attic by ὑπό + genitive (rarely by the dative alone).

*4. **Price or value**: the value of something or the price for which one gives or does anything is expressed by the genitive.

φίλος ἐστὶ χρηστὸς πολλοῦ.	A friend is worth much.
ἀπο-δίδομαι οἶνον ἀργύρου.	I sell wine for silver.
πόσου διδάσκει;	For how much does he teach?

*5. **Cause**: with verbs of emotion the genitive may denote the cause.

ἐχολωσάμην σοι δόλου.	I was angry with you because of your trickery.
ἐθαύμασε τῆς χάριτος αὐτῆς.	He marveled at her beauty.
αἰνήσω ὑμᾶς τῆς ἀρετῆς.	I will praise you for your manliness.

*6. **Time**: the partitive genitive is used to denote a time of which only a part is of interest, that is, a *time within which* an action took place.

ἦλθε τῆς νυκτός.	He came during the night.
θανοῦμαι τοῦ λοιποῦ.	I shall die in the future.

The **dative of time** denotes a definite point of time *at which* an action occurred, and usually contrasts one point of time with another.

τῇ δευτέρᾳ ἡμέρᾳ	on the second day
τρίτῳ μηνί	in the third month

The **accusative of time** implies that the action of the verb covers the entire period.

ἔμειναν ἑπτὰ ἡμέρας.	They remained seven days.

*7. **Genitive absolute**: a circumstantial participle agreeing with a noun or pronoun (not referring to a person or thing mentioned in the main clause) may stand in the genitive absolute. (Compare the ablative absolute in Latin.)

τούτων λεχθέντων, ἀν-έστησαν.	When this was said, they stood up.
οὔσης γε ἀληθείης ἔστιν ἀγάπη.	Where there is truth, there is love.

III. Dative

1. **Case expressing** the basic meanings *to, for; by, with; in, on*.
2. **Dative of cause**: §18.
*3. **Place where**: in poetry the dative alone is permitted, but in Attic prose the addition of the preposition ἐν is usually required.
*4. **Agency**: if the agent is non-living, the dative is used; if the agent is living, the dative is used only with passive verbs in the perfect or pluperfect. (Otherwise, use ὑπό + genitive.)

    ἐμοὶ πέπρακται.   It has been done by me.
    ἐπειδὴ αὐτοῖς παρ-εσκεύαστο   When it had been prepared by them

*5. **Degree of difference**: with expressions of comparison, the dative is used to mark the degree by which one thing differs from another.

    πολλαῖς ἡμέραις ὕστερον ἦλθεν.   He arrived many days later.
    πολλῷ ἀρείων ἐστίν.   He is much braver.
    κεφαλῇ ἐλάττων ἐστίν.   He is a head shorter.

*6. **Respect**: the dative is sometimes used instead of the accusative of specification. There is no noticeable difference in meaning.

    ἀσθενὴς ἦν τῷ σώματι.   He was weak in body.
    τῇ φωνῇ τραχύς ἐστιν.   He is harsh of voice.

IV. Accusative

1. **Case of the direct object**
2. **Cognate accusative**: §602.
3. **Accusative of specification**: §644.
4. **Accusative of extent**: §18.
*5. **Place to which**: In poetry the accusative alone is permitted to express place to which; in Attic prose a preposition *must* accompany the accusative.
*6. **Accusative absolute**: The participles of *impersonal* verbs are used absolutely in the accusative instead of in the genitive. (Among the common impersonal verbs are: ἔξ-εστι *it is possible*, δεῖ *it is necessary*, μέλει *it concerns*.)

    ἐξ-ὸν ἐλθεῖν, οὐκ ἤθελεν.   Although it was possible to go, he was unwilling.
    δέον αἱρεῖσθαι, τόδε αἱρῶ.   Since it is necessary to choose, I take this.

*7. **With adverbs of swearing**: νή, introducing an affirmative oath, and μά, introducing a negative oath, are followed by the accusative.

    νὴ τὸν Δία.   (yes) by Zeus!
    μὰ τοὺς θεούς.   (no) by the gods!

D. Syntax of the Verb by Constructions

Note: the numbers starred contain data not met in Homer or different from Homeric usage. Where the rule is the same as in Homeric Greek, only a reference is given to the relevant section in the *Reading Course in Homeric Greek*.

1. **Circumstantial participle**: §199
2. **Commands**:
    a. Imperative: §114
    b. Infinitive: §148
    c. Optative: §106a

*d. The aorist subjunctive may be used for negative commands.

    μὴ ποιήσῃς.   Do not do this.
    μὴ ἀπ-έλθητε.   Do not go away.

*3. **Conditions or Suppositions**: The various types of conditional sentences are arranged graphically in the following chart, and an example is given of each type in Attic Greek. Remember that temporal and relative clauses follow the same constructions as conditional clauses, ὅτε *when* and ὅς *who* taking the place of εἰ *if*. (ὅτε + ἄν = ὅταν.)

    a. **Conditional Sentences in Attic Greek**

Time	Form	Protasis ["If"- clause] (Neg. μή)	Apodosis [Conclusion] (Neg. οὐ)
Present	1. Factual	εἰ + ind. (pres./pf.)	ind. (pres./pf.)
	2. Contrary-to-fact	εἰ + impf. ind.	ἄν + impf. ind.
	3. General Supposition	ἐάν + subj.	pres. ind.
Past	4. Factual	εἰ + ind. (impf./aor./plpf.)	ind. (impf./aor./plpf.)
	5. Contrary-to-fact	εἰ + aor. ind.	ἄν + aor. ind.
	6. General Supposition	εἰ + opt.	impf. ind.
Future	7. Vivid Supposition	ἐάν + subj.	fut. ind. (or equivalent)
	8. Vague Supposition	εἰ + opt.	ἄν + opt.

    b. **Examples in Attic Greek**

1. εἰ ταῦτα λέγει, ἀληθῆ λέγει.
   If he says this, he speaks the truth.
2. εἰ ταῦτα ἔλεγε, οὐκ ἄν ἀληθῆ ἔλεγεν.
   If he were saying this (now), he would not be speaking the truth (now).
3. ἐάν τι λέγῃ (λέξῃ), ἀληθῆ λέγει.
   If he (ever) says anything, he (always) speaks the truth.
4. εἰ ταῦτα ἔλεξεν, ἀληθῆ ἔλεξεν.
   If he said this, he spoke the truth.
5. εἰ ταῦτα ἔλεξεν, οὐκ ἄν ἀληθῆ ἔλεξεν.
   If he had said this (then), he would not have spoken the truth (then).
6. εἴ τι λέγοι (λέξειεν), ἀληθῆ ἔλεγεν.
   If he (ever) said anything, he (always) spoke the truth.
7. ἐὰν ταῦτα λέγῃς (λέξῃς), ἀληθῆ λέξεις.
   If you say this, you will speak the truth.
8. εἰ ταῦτα λέγοις (λέξειας), ἀληθῆ ἄν λέγοις (λέξειας).
   If you should say this, you would speak the truth.

*4. **Deliberative questions**: The subjunctive of the first person may be used in a purely rhetorical question. Neg. μή.

    τί ποιῶμεν;   What shall we do?
    εἴπωμεν ἢ σιγῶμεν;   Shall we speak or keep silence?
    μὴ ταῦτα φῶμεν;   Shall we not say this?

5. **Expectation** (optative): §524
6. **Explanatory** (infinitive): §588
7. **Fact** (indicative): §91a
8. **Hortatory** (subjunctive): §98a
9. **Indirect discourse**: When one reports the words of another, not directly (with quotation marks) but according to sense, he uses what is called indirect discourse. Latin regularly uses but one construction for this: the accusative with infinitive. Greek, however, offers two other choices: the participial construction and ὅτι with a finite verb.

    a. Accusative with infinitive: §114.2c

  *b. Participial construction: The participle sometimes takes the place of the infinitive and is in the same tense as the infinitive would be if used. Cf. §199.

        ὁρῶμεν πάντα ἀληθῆ ὄντα.   We see that everything is true.
        οὐκ ἔγνωσαν αὐτὸν τεθνηκότα.   They did not know that he was dead.
        ἤκουσα τοὺς ἄνδρας οὐκ ἀφ-ιξομένους.   I heard that the men would not arrive.

  *c. ὅτι with a finite verb: this construction is very close to the English usage. After a primary main verb, the original mood and tense of the dependent verb are retained.

        λέγει ὅτι οἱ ἄνδρες οὐκ ἀφ-ίξονται.   He says that the men will not arrive.
        λέγει ὅτι οἱ ἄνδρες οὐκ ἀφ-ίκοντο.   He says that the men did not arrive.

After a secondary main verb, the dependent verb may sometimes be changed to the optative, the tense remaining the same if possible. The negative always remains the same.

        ἔλεξεν ὅτι οἱ ἄνδρες οὐκ ἀφ-ίξοιντο.   He said that the men would not arrive.
        ἔλεξεν ὅτι οἱ ἄνδρες οὐκ ἀφ-ίκοιντο.   He said that the men had not arrived.

Note: which construction should be used in a given situation is a question that cannot be answered by any general rule. However,

    (a) Most verbs of *thinking* and *believing* take acc. + inf.
    (b) Verbs of *saying* frequently take the ὅτι construction.
    (c) Verbs of *knowing* and *perceiving* often take the participle.

10. **Indirect questions**: §§214, 463

*11. **Object clauses**: These are clauses which are used as the objects of verbs such as *I strive that, I take care that, I plan that*, etc. In Homer they take ὅπως with the purpose construction. In Attic also they may take the purpose construction, but more frequently they take ὅπως with the **future indicative** even after a secondary verb. Neg. μή.

    βουλεύομαι ὅπως ταῦτα ποιήσομεν.   I plan that we shall do this.
    ἐβουλευόμην ὅπως μὴ ταῦτα ποιήσομεν.   I planned that we should not do this.

12. **Potential** (optative): §285b

13. **Purpose**: There are four ways of expressing purpose. For example: This man sent (sends) a friend to save us.
    a. Subjunctive or optative: οὗτος ὁ ἀνὴρ πέμπει φίλον ὅπως σώζῃ ἡμᾶς.
    οὗτος ὁ ἀνὴρ ἔπεμψε φίλον ἵνα σώζοι ἡμᾶς.
    b. Infinitive: οὗτος ὁ ἀνὴρ ἔπεμψε φίλον σώζειν ἡμᾶς.
    c. Future participle: οὗτος ὁ ἀνὴρ ἔπεμψε φίλον σώσοντα ἡμᾶς.
    *d. ὅς *who* with future indicative: οὗτος ὁ ἀνὴρ ἔπεμψε φίλον ὅς σώσει ἡμᾶς.

*14. **Result**: To express the result of an action, Greek has two constructions: ὥστε with the infinitive and ὥστε with the indicative. The main clause frequently has such demonstrative words as οὕτως *thus, so*; τοιοῦτος *such*; τοσοῦτος *so great*.
    a. If the main clause has the emphatic idea and the result clause is added primarily to bring out this idea by showing its natural or anticipated result, though not necessarily its actual result, ὥστε is used with the inf. Neg. μή.
        ἡ θύελλα τοσαύτη ἦν ὥστε ἀπ-όλεσαι τὴν ναῦν.   The storm was so great as to destroy the boat.
        (The storm was violent enough to destroy the boat, though perhaps actually it did not.)
    b. If the result clause expresses an important <u>fact</u> for which the main clause helps to account, ὥστε is used with the indicative. Neg. οὐ.
        ἡ θύελλα τοσαύτη ἦν ὥστε ἀπ-ώλεσε τὴν ναῦν.   The storm was so great that it destroyed the boat.
        (The boat was sunk— so great was the storm.)

*15. **Supplementary participle**: The participle may be used to supplement the meaning of three particular verbs to such an extent that the participle itself carries the main idea. The three verbs are: τυγχάνω *I happen*; λανθάνω *I elude, I escape (someone's notice)*; φθάνω *I anticipate*.
    ἐτύγχανε παρ-ών.   He was there by chance.
    (He happened being there.)
    ἔλαθον εἰσ-ελθόντες.   They came in secretly.
    (They escaped notice coming in.)
    ἔφθασε τὸν βασιλέα εἰς τὴν πόλιν ἀφ-ικόμενος.   He arrived at the city before the king.
    (He anticipated the king, coming to the city.)

*16. **Verbs of fearing**:
    a. Fear to do something: infinitive. Neg. μή.
        φοβοῦμαι ἀδικεῖν.   I fear to do wrong.
        φοβοῦμαι μὴ εἴκειν.   I am afraid not to yield.
    b. Fear that something will happen: after primary main verb, use μή with subjunctive; after secondary main verb, use μή with subjunctive or optative. Neg. μὴ οὐ.
        φοβοῦμαι μὴ (οὐ) γένηται.   I fear it may (not) happen.
        ἐφοβούμην μὴ (οὐ) γένοιτο or γένηται.   I feared it might (not) happen.

17. **Wishes**: in Homer, wishes both possible and impossible of fulfilment are expressed by the optative, often with εἰ, εἴθε, or εἰ γάρ. In Attic the two kinds of wishes are carefully distinguished.
   a. Possible wishes are expressed by the optative; εἴθε or εἰ γάρ may be added. Neg. μή.
      (εἴθε, εἰ γάρ) ἔλθοι.   May he come!
   *b. Impossible wishes have two constructions.
      (1) Past tense of the indicative: imperfect for present time; aorist for past time. εἴθε or εἰ γάρ must be added. Neg. μή.
         εἴθε μὴ ἦν οὕτως μέγας.   Would that he were not so large!
         εἰ γὰρ θεὸν ἀληθῶς ἐφιλήσαμεν.   If only we had really loved God!
      (2) ὤφελον *I ought* with the infinitive: present for present time; aorist for past time. Neg. μή.
         ὤφελεν Ὀδυσσεὺς παρ-εῖναι.   Would that Odysseus were here!
         μήποτε ὠφέλομεν λιπεῖν οἶκον.   Would that we had never left home!

E. Syntax of the Verb by Moods

   I. INDICATIVE (tenses indicate time, as well as kind, of action)
   1. Conditions: neg. in protasis ["if" clause] μή; in apodosis [conclusion] οὐ.
      a. Factual: §91a.
      b. Contrary-to-fact: §91b
         *(1) Present time: εἰ + impf. ind. in protasis; ἄν with impf. ind. in apodosis.
            εἰ ταῦτα ἔλεγον, οὐκ ἂν ἀληθῆ ἔλεγεν.
            If he were saying this (now), he would not be speaking the truth (now).
         *(2) Past time: εἰ + aor. ind. in protasis; ἄν with aor. ind. in apodosis.
            εἰ ταῦτα ἔλεξεν, οὐκ ἂν ἀληθῆ ἔλεξεν.
            If he had said this (then), he would not have spoken the truth (then).
   2. **Fact**: §91.
   *3. **Indirect discourse**: ὅτι with a finite verb may be used after verbs of <u>saying</u>, etc. After a primary main verb, the original mood and tense of the dependent verb are retained.
         λέγει ὅτι οἱ ἄνδρες οὐκ ἀφ-ίξονται.   He says that the men will not arrive.
         λέγει ὅτι οἱ ἄνδρες οὐκ ἀφ-ίκοντο.   He says that the men did not arrive.
   4. **Indirect questions**: §§214, 463
   *5. **Object clauses**: These are clauses that are used as the objects of verbs such as *I strive that, I take care that, I plan that*, etc. In Homer they take ὅπως with the purpose construction. In Attic also they may take the purpose construction, but more frequently they take ὅπως with the **future indicative** even after a secondary verb. Neg. μή.
         βουλεύομαι ὅπως ταῦτα ποιήσομεν.   I plan that we shall do this.
         ἐβουλευόμην ὅπως μὴ ταῦτα ποιήσομεν.   I planned that we should not do this.
   *6. **Purpose**: ὅς *who* is sometimes used with the future indicative to express purpose.
         οὗτος ὁ ἀνὴρ ἔπεμψε φίλον ὅς σώσει ἡμᾶς.   This man sent a friend to save us.
   *7. **Result**: To emphasize the actual result of an action, ὥστε is used with the indicative. Neg. οὐ.
         ἡ θύελλα τοσαύτη ἦν ὥστε ἀπ-ώλεσε τὴν ναῦν.   The storm was so great that it destroyed the boat.
   *8. **Wishes**: Impossible wishes may be expressed by a past tense of the indicative: imperfect for present time; aorist for past time. εἴθε or εἰ γάρ must be added. Neg. μή.
         εἴθε μὴ ἦν οὕτως μέγας.   Would that he were not so large!
         εἰ γὰρ θεὸν ἀληθῶς ἐφιλήσαμεν.   If only we had really loved God!

II. **SUBJUNCTIVE** (tenses indicate kind of action, not time)

*1. **Commands**: The aorist subjunctive may be used for negative commands. Neg. μή.

    μὴ ποιήσῃς.   Do not do this.

    μὴ ἀπ-έλθητε.   Do not go away.

2. **Conditions**: Neg. in protasis μή; in apodosis οὐ.

    a. General supposition in present time: ἐάν + subj. in protasis; pres. ind. in apodosis.

        ἐάν τι λέγῃ (λέξῃ), ἀληθῆ λέγει.   If he (ever) says anything, he (always) speaks the truth.

    b. Vivid future supposition: ἐάν + subj. in protasis; fut. ind. (or equivalent) in apodosis.

        ἐὰν ταῦτα λέγῃς (λέξῃς), ἀληθῆ λέξεις.   If you say this, you will speak the truth.

*3. **Deliberative questions**: The subjunctive of the first person may be used in a purely rhetorical question. Neg. μή.

    τί ποιῶμεν;   What shall we do?

    εἴπωμεν ἢ σιγῶμεν;   Shall we speak or keep silence?

    μὴ ταῦτα φῶμεν;   Shall we not say this?

4. **Hortatory**: §98a

5. **Purpose**: §98b

*6. **Verbs of fearing**: After a primary (sometimes after a secondary) main verb take μή with the subjunctive. Neg. μὴ οὐ.

    φοβοῦμαι μὴ (οὐ) γένηται.   I fear it may (not) happen.

III. **OPTATIVE** (tenses indicate kind of action, not time)

1. **Commands**: §106a

2. **Conditions**: Neg. in protasis μή; in apodosis οὐ.

    a. General supposition in past time: §480

   *b. Vague future supposition: εἰ + opt. in "if"-clause; ἄν with opt. in conclusion. Cf. §285a.

        εἰ ταῦτα λέγοις (λέξειας), ἀληθῆ ἂν λέγοις (λέξειας).   If you should say this, you would speak the truth.

3. **Expectation**: §524.

*4. **Indirect discourse**: ὅτι with a finite verb may be used after verbs of *saying*, etc. After a secondary main verb, the dependent verb may sometimes be changed to the optative, the tense remaining the same if possible. The negative always remains unchanged.

    ἔλεξεν ὅτι οἱ ἄνδρες οὐκ ἀφ-ίξοιντο.   He said that the men would not arrive.

    ἔλεξεν ὅτι οἱ ἄνδρες οὐκ ἀφ-ίκοιντο.   He said that the men had not arrived.

5. **Indirect questions**: §§214, 463

6. **Potential**: §285b

7. **Purpose**: §106b

*8. **Verbs of fearing**: After a secondary main verb take μή with the optative. Neg. μὴ οὐ.

    ἐφοβούμην μὴ (οὐ) γένοιτο.   I feared it might (not) happen.

9. **Wishes**: Possible wishes are expressed by the optative. εἴθε or εἰ γάρ may be added. Neg. μή.

    (εἴθε, εἰ γὰρ) ἔλθοι.   May he come!

IV. **IMPERATIVE** (tenses indicate kind of action, not time)

1. **Commands**: §114.

V. INFINITIVE (tenses indicate kind of action except in indirect discourse)

1. **Commands**: §148.
2. **Explanatory**: §588
3. **Indirect discourse** (Accusative with infinitive): §114.2c
4. **Purpose**: §588
*5. **Result**: ὥστε with the infinitive is used to express the natural or anticipated result of an action, though not necessarily its actual result. Neg. μή.

    ἡ θύελλα τοσαύτη ἦν ὥστε ἀπ-ολέσαι τὴν ναῦν. The storm was so great as to destroy the boat.

*6. **Wishes**: Impossible wishes may be expressed by ὤφελον *I ought* with the infinitive: present for present time; aorist for past time. Neg. μή.

    ὤφελεν Ὀδυσσεὺς παρ-εῖναι.   Would that Odysseus were here!
    μήποτε ὠφέλομεν λιπεῖν οἶκον.   Would that we had never left home!

VI. PARTICIPLE (tenses indicate time of action)

1. **Circumstantial participle**: §199
*2. **Indirect discourse**: The participle sometimes takes the place of the infinitive and is in the same tense as the infinitive would be if used.

    ὁρῶμεν πάντα ἀληθῆ ὄντα.   We see that everything is true.
    οὐκ ἔγνωσαν αὐτὸν τεθνηκότα.   They did not know that he was dead.

3. **Purpose**: The participle (regularly the future) may be used to express purpose.

    οὗτος ὁ ἀνὴρ ἔπεμψε φίλον σώσοντα ἡμᾶς.   This man sent a friend to save us.

*4. **Supplementary participle**: The participle may be used to supplement the meaning of three particular verbs to such an extent that the participle itself carries the main idea. The three verbs are: τυγχάνω *I happen*; λανθάνω *I elude, I escape (someone's notice)*; φθάνω *I anticipate*.

    ἐτύγχανε παρ-ών.   He was there by chance.
        (He happened being there.)
    ἔλαθον εἰσ-ελθόντες.   They came in secretly.
        (They escaped notice coming in.)
    ἔφθασε τὸν βασιλέα εἰς τὴν πόλιν ἀφ-ικόμενος.   He arrived at the city before the king.
        (He anticipated the king, coming to the city.)

Part V
VOCABULARY

Of the more than one thousand words you have memorized in the *Reading Course in Homeric Greek*, nearly ninety percent undergo no changes in passing over into Attic prose. Of those that do change in Attic Greek, practically all will be easily recognized. Besides, even these words frequently occur in their older form in Attic poetry. Here is a breakdown of the words you have learned which are different in Attic prose.

A. About forty are adjectives of the 1st and 2nd declensions that differ only in taking α in the feminine instead of η. This is in keeping with the Attic rule that α is used after ε, ι, or ρ. For example:

δίκαιος, -η, -ον = δίκαιος, -α, -ον   γλυκερός, -ή, -όν = γλυκερός, -ά, -όν

B. Twenty-three other words also change η to α. Of these, notice that twelve are 1st declension nouns whose stems end in ε, ι, or ρ.

ἀγγελίη = ἀγγελία	κνίση = κνῖσα
ἀγορή = ἀγορά	Ἀθήνη = Ἀθηνᾶ
ἀληθείη = ἀλήθεια	βρώμη = βρῶμα
βασιλείη = βασιλείᾱ	κάρη = κάρᾱ
βίη = βία	κρητήρ = κρᾱτήρ
θύρη = θύρα	νηῦς = ναῦς
κονίη = κονία	ἰητρός = ἰᾱτρός
μελίη = μελία	ἔμπης = ἔμπᾱς
πάτρη = πάτρᾱ	λίην = λίαν
πέτρη = πέτρα	ἀήρ, ἠέρος = ἀήρ, ἀέρος
πυρή = πυρά	(ἀράομαι) ἀρήσομαι = ἀράσομαι
σχεδίη = σχεδία	

C. Forty words undergo contraction or shortening when passing into Attic.

1. Adjectives in -εος usually contract.

ἀργύρεος, -η, -ον = ἀργυροῦς, -ᾶ, -οῦν	χάλκεος, -η, -ον = χαλκοῦς, -ῆ, -οῦν
πορφύρεος, -η, -ον = πορφυροῦς, -ᾶ, -οῦν	χρύσεος, -η, -ον = χρυσοῦς, -ῆ, -οῦν
σιδήρεος, -η, -ον = σιδηροῦς, -ᾶ, -οῦν	κυάνεος, -η, -ον = κυανοῦς, -ῆ, -οῦν

2. Attic often shortens ου to ο.

γόνυ, γούνατος = γόνυ, γόνατος	νοῦσος = νόσος
δόρυ, δούρατος = δόρυ, δόρατος	οὐδός = ὀδός
κούρη = κόρη	οὖλος = ὅλος
μοῦνος = μόνος	

3. ει is shortened in the following words:

ἀεικής = αἰκής	εἵνεκα = ἕνεκα
ἀείρω = αἴρω	εἴρομαι = ἔρομαι
ξείνιον = ξένιον	φαείνω = φαίνω
ξεῖνος = ξένος	

4. These words contract according to the rules previously learned.

ἀέκων = ἄκων	ὀστέον = ὀστοῦν
ἀοιδή = ᾠδή	ῥόος = ῥοῦς
(ἐ)έργω = εἴργω	φάος = φῶς
ἠέλιος = ἥλιος	Ποσειδάων = Ποσειδῶν
νόος = νοῦς	

5. Other words that are shortened:

αἰεί = ἀεί	δένδρεον = δένδρον
αἰετός = ἀετός	ἐννέπω = ἐνέπω
κλαίω = κλάω	ἐννοσίγαιος = ἐνοσίγαιος
αὐτάρ = ἀτάρ	ἑός, ή, όν = ὅς, ἥ, ὄν
γαῖα = γῆ	κληΐς = κλείς

D. Double sigma often changes to double tau in Attic.

θάλασσα = θάλαττα	φυλάσσω = φυλάττω
θάσσων = θάττων	πρήσσω = πράττω
πλήσσω = πλήττω	(σφάζω = σφάττω)

E. A few words suffer what is called a metathesis of quantity, that is, the transposition of the quantity of two vowels. Sometimes consonants are similarly changed.

ἦος = ἕως	νηός = νεώς
λᾱός = λεώς	κραδίη = καρδία

F. These 28 words fit into no particular classification.

ἀέξω = αὔξω	Ἠώς = Ἕως
(αἰνέω) αἰνήσω = αἰνέσω	θέμις, θέμιστος = θέμις, θέμιτος
ἀλωή = ἅλως	Θήβη = Θῆβαι
ἅμαξα = ἅμαξα	ἰθύς = εὐθύς
ἀπείρων = ἄπειρος	κεῖνος = ἐκεῖνος
(ἁρπάζω) ἁρπάξω = ἁρπάσω	κεῖσε = ἐκεῖσε
αὖτις = αὖθις	κιχάνω = κιγχάνω
(γίγνομαι) γέγαα = γέγονα	ὅθι = οὗ
δεξιτερός = δεξιός	πεῖραρ = πέρας
ἐλεαίρω = ἐλεέω	πεύθομαι = πυνθάνομαι
ἔρος = ἔρως	(ὀλλύω) ὀλέσω = ὀλῶ
ζώω = ζάω	τάμνω = τέμνω
ἦμαρ = ἡμέρα	χρώς, χροός = χρώς, χρωτός
ἐπι-μάσσομαι = ἐπι-μάσομαι	ἐΰσσελμος = ἐΰσελμος

Answers to Exercises on Page 11

Exercise on 1st and 2nd declensions

1. ἡδονῶν
2. νεανίαν
3. νοῦν
4. πέτρᾳ
5. χαλκᾶς
6. ἀργυρᾶ
7. εἰρήναις
8. ποιουσῶν
9. ποιουμένου
10. οὐτώσαις

Exercise on 3rd declension

1. πλείονας or πλείους
2. δυσμενῆ
3. γηρῶν
4. φύσεως
5. ὀξέων
6. ποιοῦντι
7. τοκεῖς
8. νῆες
9. ἄστεως
10. παῖδα
11. εὐρέα
12. ἄλγη
13. ἄρειον
14. ἰχθῦς
15. χθόνα
16. μηκῶν
17. βοῦς
18. οὑτῶσι
19. σώμασι
20. βασιλέας
21. μελιηδῆ
22. διοτρεψοῦς
23. ὠκεῖς
24. ποιμένα
25. τοκέως
26. πατράσι
27. γήρᾳ
28. παχεῖς
29. ἄστη
30. κράτους